Every Day Is
SUNDAY

Every Day Is
SUNDAY

Ralph Schoenstein

LITTLE, BROWN AND COMPANY
BOSTON · TORONTO

FIRST EDITION

*All the names of the real people in this book
have been changed to protect their privacy.*

LIBRARY OF CONGRESS CATALOGING-IN-PUBLICATION DATA

Schoenstein, Ralph, 1933–
Every day is Sunday.

1. Retirement communities — United States —
Anecdotes, facetiae, satire, etc. I. Title.
HQ1063.S34   1986   646.7′9   85-18075
ISBN 0-316-77428-6

BP

Designed by Jeanne F. Abboud

*Published simultaneously in Canada
by Little, Brown & Company (Canada) Limited*

PRINTED IN THE UNITED STATES OF AMERICA

For Judy, Jill, Eve-Lynn, and Lori
The best community of all

CONTENTS

Grow old along with me.
The best is yet to be.

ROBERT BROWNING

Go Where, Middle-aged Man?

PREFACE

"Daddy, how old will you be when I'm ninety?" said my daughter Lori, who was eight.

"A hundred thirty-three," I blithely replied.

"Will we still be able to play touch football?"

"I'll have to do mostly passing," I said. "Tight ends lose a couple of steps after ninety-five."

And then a discomforting thought filled the misty mind of a man who felt himself to be America's oldest adolescent: what *will* I be doing at ninety-five in this land obsessed by age, where numbers are mindlessly tacked to all names:

Ralph Schoenstein, 51, and his daughter Lori, 8, were trying to catch a bunny, 2, when Lori tripped on the root of a tree, 106.

I did not plan to shoot myself at sixty-five, an option suggested by the Pepsi Generation, but where *should* I be then and what should I be doing? Was there one best place in which I should break down in my golden years? Should I stay in the untamed North and wind up in a room over my daughter's garage? Or should I head for a southern adult community, a leisure village, and go gentle into that good night with a shuffleboard stick in my hand?

For centuries, older Eskimos and Indians who found themselves a burden to their families were allowed to go off to die. America today, however, encourages its older citizens to go off into sunny internment. We invented this segregation in 1960, when a developer named Del Webb built Sun City, Arizona, which is now the size of Peekskill, New York; and we began to export it in 1984, when Japanese developers studied the leisure villages of New Jersey so they could build the first Rising Sun City. And now I was pondering whether I should also be planning my escape. I knew that some of my contemporaries, men and women in their early fifties, were already considering moves to places where no children or change of season was allowed, where the people passed flawless days comparing bypass stories, bond prices, and beautiful grandchildren.

Or *did* they? I had just superficial knowledge of the leisure village from talking to my mother and mother-in-law, both of whom lived near Florida's four Century Villages, which now held forty thousand people. I did know that the leisure village was the major social revolution of our time, and I heard its message in ads and commercials constantly calling to me: Leave the cold and the crime, lower your mortgage and blood pressure, and join all the enlightened folks at Leisure World and Sun City, at Rainbow Village and Happy Dale, at Euphoria Gardens and Rebate Estates. I already had turned fifty-one, but fifty-one did not mean what it used to: fifty-one was no longer over the hill because the hill had been moved, a relocation that made me wonder about the wisdom of moving to an adult hothouse in Florida, Arizona, and California. The leisure village seemed inconsistent with the dramatic extension of the American prime; but perhaps the prime now belonged there. I had to find out; I had to go to some of these places and decide if I should consider someday joining more than a million other dropouts who no longer lived in a world where people were shooting each other down after shooting themselves up.

I had heard many appealing things about the leisure village: that life there was less expensive, free from stress, and even longer. And long, cheap, stressless life just happened to be something I could use. I often awoke at three in the morning, what the Russians call the Hour of the Wolf, but I was an American chicken, terrified by the chaos and cruelty of life. As much as I loved a life of improvisation in the mainstream of the world, part of me now was yearning for a world of safety, continuous sense, and predictably pleasant routine. Was the leisure village the answer for me? Was the leisure village making Robert Browning right? Or was Browning still a lyrical fool?

With Screws
in the Swan

PART I

"I *hate* those brown spots!" said the radio voice as I began to seek the bluebird of golden age happiness in my own backyard. I was driving to Clearbrook, a community for people over forty-eight, in Cranbury, New Jersey, just a few miles from my home in Princeton. "Those brown spots on my hands and neck are so *unattractive.*"

And while an announcer told this poor woman that she could change color in the sunset with Porcelana Fade Cream, I took my right hand off the wheel and checked again for my own brown spots, dreading the appearance of the first, which I planned to cover with beige Magic Marker. Once again, I envied black men. Once again, I found myself guilty of the same idiotic obsession with age that possessed most of my countrymen. I could not make myself forget that I was heading for Spot City.

". . . and now my spots are fading and they no longer bother me," the former leopard was saying, while I wondered how much time I devoted each day to fearing aging and death. Even though I was three years over the minimum age, would I still be barred from an adult community because of my inability to become an adult and accept the natural course of things?

A few days ago, Lori had told me, "Daddy, please don't die."

"I'll try not to, honey," I had said. "The law of averages is against it, but *somebody* has to be first."

Lori, my blessed afterthought.

When I was a boy, I had always known the ages of the sisters and brothers of my friends — either four years older or four years younger — because parents in those days seemed to have their children with all the spontaneity of presidential elections. And my wife Judy and I had also been traditional breeders when we began: our daughter Jill was born at the start of the 1960 presidential campaign and our daughter Eve-Lynn was born during the primaries of 1964. When we skipped the elections of '68 and '72, we presumed we would have no more candidates. "A wife and two children" had a nice ring to me, as if I were being true to the tables of Mutual of Omaha.

And then, the week of Jimmy Carter's nomination in 1976, came Lori. In 1984, I was a man of fifty-one with a wife of forty-six and three daughters whose ages sounded like a winning bingo card. Since no children were allowed to live in the leisure villages, I wouldn't be able to move into one until Lori was self-sufficient, fifteen or twenty years from now; but by then, I might have to skip the leisure village and move directly to a fashionable respirator. Moreover, before Lori became self-sufficient, I should take a crack at it myself, for in the last twenty-five years

I had signed my name to fourteen books and thirteen loans; and most of the loans had stayed in print longer than most of the books. Only Judy's teaching salary had enabled us to keep our tenuous hold on the middle class.

The car radio had changed to the haunting irony of "Time in a Bottle," Jim Croce's wish just before his own time had run out, and I opened my mouth and took a long breath. Too often these days the passage of time, the change in family faces from old photographs to new, had left me gasping in despair. "But at my back I always hear/Time's wingèd chariot hurrying near." If time's wingèd chariot were only a canoe!

Turning off the radio, I began to play mental tapes of random sweet moments from the last forty years, trying in dismay to figure out where those years had gone and what they had meant. Even my recent achievements, such as having two essays in *Newsweek* and one in *The New York Times* in less than a year, had already vanished like the vapors talked of in *The Tempest,* leaving me to wonder what they — or *anything* — meant. And where had my father gone after his death in 1974? If there *was* an afterlife, had he been spending the last decade talking to his relatives? This thought depressed me too because he had never been able to stand them.

I might not have been right for an adult community, but I was perfect for the Seniors Club of the New Jersey Neuropsychiatric Institute.

As I drove through Cranbury on the road to Clearbrook, the landscape started a mental tape of my driving Eve-Lynn to a camp near here on a summer day when she was Lori's age, when I still carried her once in a while and puberty was just another word she couldn't spell.

But enough; no more melancholy yearning for the past when such a splendid future beckoned me. *The best years of your life begin at Clearbrook,* the ad had said. With homes starting at $66,000 and a monthly maintenance of just $125 that *included* sewer tax.

When I reached the entrance to Clearbrook, I found a gate house with a bar across the road and a sign that said

RESIDENTS ONLY. CARD-OPERATED
GATE CLOSES AFTER EACH VEHICLE.

"I want to see Clearbrook," I told the guard.

"You want the sales office," he said. "Turn right and go down the road to a sign for the models."

Following his direction, I soon came to the office that ran both Clearbrook and an adjoining community called Rossmoor, where a sign said

WELCOME TO NEW JERSEY'S
FINEST ADULT COMMUNITIES

I walked inside and a sandy-haired salesman in a gold jacket intercepted me and said in a British accent, "May I help you?"

"Yes, my wife and I are thinking of buying here," I replied. "May I go into the community and look around?"

"Not by yourself — security, you know — but our van can take you there. Why don't you look at the models next door first? They're all Rossmoor colonials — and the Massachusetts is still available for only $77,900, though I'm afraid that'll be much higher soon."

I thanked him, accepted a brochure, filled out a prospective buyer card, and then went out to the Massachusetts. Once inside this two-story colonial, I needed to use the toilet, but the lid of the seat was bolted down. I had entered a graciously paranoid world. The sound of a toilet, however, would have jarred the gleaming stillness of this house, with its plush carpeting, its dramatic floodlighting, and its breakfast table set so elegantly for two with fine china, embroidered napkins, and crystal fruit cups. I pictured Judy and me sitting here, sipping our prune juice and jesting softly about the new electrified fence.

On the living-room wall of the Massachusetts, a plaque said

Some of the items in these homes may be
available at additional cost, for example:
PATIO ENCLOSURE
FURNITURE AND ACCESSORIES
WALL COVERINGS
SPECIAL LIGHTING
WINDOW TREATMENTS
MIRRORED DOORS / WALLS
UPGRADED APPLIANCES
UPGRADED FLOOR COVERING

A few minutes later, I walked down a lane to one of the contemporary models, a ranch house called Masterlodge, whose doormat said

WE'RE INVOLVED IN SAVING ENERGY

In the kitchen of the Masterlodge, as I walked past laminated counters, a frost-free refrigerator, a self-cleaning oven, and a stainless-steel sink with a one-lever faucet, I was suddenly startled to see pasted over the entire big rectangular window a photograph of the outdoors, the first picture window that truly deserved its name. The photo was dominated by a big cherry tree found at the Jefferson Memorial but not at Clearbrook, which had the landscaping of Fort Dix. Gazing at this remarkable window, I felt myself drifting farther and farther from reality. Clearbrook itself was a kind of Hollywood set, and this window was a set *within* a set.

At a model next door called the Timberline, I met a couple who were abandoning New Brunswick.

"We're buying this one," said the woman, who seemed to be in her late sixties. "What about you?"

"I like the Masterlodge," I told her. "The kitchen has a great view of Washington."

"Oh, that's not *available;* they were all snapped up. At eighty-nine thousand, they were a steal. Have you seen the Devon or the Cambridge?"

"No, but I'd like to; a nice British ring. Are they Tudor?"

"Sort of Contemporary Tudor," she said, "with a feeling of Cape Cod. If you want to see them, you have to take the van into the community."

"I know. They don't want people like me wandering around."

"You know, you don't look forty-eight."

"Thanks, but I've passed it. But my wife hasn't. Nor our eight-year-old. You see, I'm looking a bit down the road."

"You couldn't move in with a child, of course, but he *could* live with you for a hundred twenty days a year."

"Lori would like that. And the rest of the time, she could travel."

"This place is pretty liberal about children. They can use all the facilities when they visit, as long as they don't hog the tennis courts and they're not too wild. Wildness is for the outside."

After finishing my tour of the Timberline, one of whose highlights was what the brochure called "a marbelized vanity top with integrated bowl," I went outside and began talking to a woman of about seventy, who wore pink pedal pushers, Adidas, and a sweater whose collar was edged with pearls. Just as her outfit was lost between Miami Beach and Madison Square Garden, her hair was also uncertain whether it wanted to be blond or gray. As we talked, I learned that she was a widow who had moved from Florida to Clearbrook last year.

"I came back to New Jersey when my first grandchild was born in Princeton," she said. "I didn't come back just to be a grandmother. I also take courses in art history at Rutgers, I work with children at the Y, and I sew. Still, there's nothing like a family to heal you; it's the kids who keep us going."

I realized now that if Judy and I moved from Princeton to this place, we would be able to take advantage of all the cultural things in the Princeton area. In fact, it would be a good time to start.

"Are there any stores or markets here?" I said.

"No, you have to go outside."

"So you need a car."

"Well, there are buses to the shopping centers, but you do need a car. Anyway, there's so much to *do* here that you think less and less about leaving. You can't *believe* the activities. And I've got my *independence*. You see, living with your children — that's old-fashioned now."

When she left this old-fashioned man, I walked over

to the Clearbrook van, introduced myself to the driver, and began my own exploration of the village, a place that told people to come "when you're no longer tied down to children, a house, a school system, or a community." With sadness, I remembered how stirringly all these shackles were saluted by Sinatra in a song called "The House I Live In."

"How many homes in Clearbrook?" I asked the driver as we moved through the main checkpoint, where the guard forgot to search me for marked canasta decks.

"Around fourteen hundred," he said. "And you can't buy 'em this cheap outside."

When we started passing the homes, a variety of one- and two-story models, I saw that they sat with surgical neatness on lawns that could have been golf greens. Not a single piece of trash was in sight. Judy and I and the girls had always lived in a lovable mess. What traumatic neatness life here might be!

"I guess there's no crime around here," I said.

"Are you kidding?" the driver replied. "None of them goddam animals in *here*. Really terrific security. Every- thing's under control."

Control: that was the question, bigger than to be or not to be. No question had tortured me more: How much of my life was in my control and how much in the mind- less control of capricious luck, perverse fate, or an un- fathomable God? Even at the Macy parade on Thanksgiving Day with Lori, I sometimes felt like a balloon lost in the winds of an indifferent and absurd universe.

"Is it true that somebody in the world is killed every day?" Lori had asked me, and I was anguished by her rotten arithmetic. Every time I picked up a newspaper,

I got ink on my hands and a chill in my soul from the rundown of the world's random horror: A six-year-old boy is accidentally shot to death by a cop, a school flagpole falls on a girl of ten and crushes her, a mother drowns trying to save her daughter, a boy's father sets him on fire, and a drunken driver kills seven people at a bus stop. However, today's banner headline in *The Clearbrook Courier* says

Shopping Center Denied;
Guardian Weighs Appeal

The *world* may have had no design, but the Guardian Development Corporation did. Could I blame these people for taking refuge in its cocoon? And their refuge was profound indeed, for as I rode through the clean curving streets, I was suddenly struck by the old question: What's wrong with this picture? And the answer was: There were *no people*. Incredibly, no one was walking around. Since this was noon of a spectacularly beautiful late summer day, the eerie emptiness was even more bewildering.

"Where are all the people?" I asked the driver.

"Inside," he said.

Hiding from all the randomness. Perhaps a world with two dimensions was better than a world with three. It was *dangerous* out there. Of course, even in here, the ultimate danger, the Appointment in Samarra, still came to every hiding place: the entire *Letters* page of *The Courier* carried messages of gratitude for either good wishes during a sickness or condolences for a death. I thought of Lori's touching fear that I might drift into an official elderly state.

"Daddy, I don't like your gray hair," she had said. "It

makes you look old. Can't you change it back to black again?"

"Oh, *that* doesn't make me *old*," I had lamely replied. "*I'll* show you who's old. Race you to the mailbox!"

And while I was running, just hard enough to beat her by a couple of strides, I wondered if pressure from her or from my own vanity would ever lead me to the Clairol fountain of youth. Perhaps I could color-coordinate the dye on my head with the dye on my spots.

The driver and I continued moving through the anti-septic streets until we came to the clubhouse, the heart of every adult community, where I went inside and heard Jerome Kern softly sounding from above. On a bulletin board there were notices for the Art Appreciation Club, the Walking Club, the Stamp Club, the Bowling League, ballroom dancing, a call for female pool shooters, and a lecture on "The Effect of the Nuclear Arms Race on Children and Families." Turning to a white-haired man in a Mets cap, I said, "I think I'd like to hear the lecture on nuclear arms."

"They're all fun," he replied.

"You belong to any of these clubs?"

"No, I play bridge."

"That's nice."

"But I'm losing my game."

"Why?"

"The players keep dying."

Brooding on how mortality was shuffling the card room, I started walking down the hall, past a little library, where a man with an alligator shirt and New York Yankee cap was deep in *USA Today;* past a golf tournament board, where a woman with orange hair was telling a friend,

"Can you *believe* such a small world? Meeting Millie at a Copenhagen *shul*"; past the big card room itself, where several tables were full of female bridge players; and past the Health Care Center, where a sign on the door said

YES, WE'LL DO YOUR BLOOD PRESSURE

When I reached the art room, I went inside and was quickly confronted by a big-boned man with wild white hair, who said, "How did *you* get in here?"

"I'm just looking," I told him, startled by this jumpiness in Eden. "I'm thinking of moving here someday."

"You'll love it!" cried a beefy woman in a smock, who was painting a ceramic candy dish at a table nearby. "Do you like to make things out of clay?"

"I'm afraid I'm not very good at clay," I said, thinking, *Maybe I could be assigned to license plates or the laundry.*

"We can teach you," said the man with wild hair. "I taught this at Stuyvesant High."

"I almost *flunked* this at Stuyvesant High," I said, trying to remember him.

"This whole place is adult education," said the beefy woman, "and nobody flunks. Come over here, I'll show you how we — my God, you're all skin and bones; don't you *eat?*"

She was showing such warmth to a stranger that I wondered if this warmth was a temperature common to leisure villages. But even if it were, did I want to fill my autumnal days making dishes for M&Ms?

"I don't think I'd be too good in this class," I told her, "unless you numbered the pieces of clay. I'd have to take something else, like glassblowing. I'm better with bubbles than pots."

"We got a class for *everything,*" she said. "I'm only here on Tuesdays. Other days I play the recorder, do folk dancing, and French."

It seemed that the leisure village was where the liberal arts were taking their last stand in a high-tech world. However, I had already been to two of the best liberal arts colleges in America, and I had come out of them so ethereal that I hadn't held a job for twenty-five years.

The possibility of doing postgraduate work at Clearbrook, perhaps majoring in finger painting or quoits, was something I pondered as I returned to the van, where I told the driver to take me back to the office.

On this trip, I saw some street life at last: a woman, who was at least sixty in both age and pounds overweight, was jogging down the road in a bright blue sweatsuit. Young joggers had always depressed me with their pious trendiness and their solemn self-canonization, but I was touched by this fat woman, bravely flopping down the road.

When the van pulled into its parking space at the office, I was startled to hear the sound of distant church bells.

"Is there a church on the grounds?" I asked the driver.

"That's from Rossmoor," he said. "There's a lotta Jews there, so they got a church too."

"But Jewish churches don't have *bells.*" I had not come out of my bar mitzvah totally uninformed.

"Listen, I dunno much about Jews. I just know if you want Jews, take Rossmoor. If you want Americans, take Clearbrook."

His sociological acumen made me realize that I had seen no blacks, Hispanics, or Orientals on the grounds, even though many in all three groups could have afforded

WITH SCREWS IN THE SWAN   —   15

an $80,000 home. The homogeneity here was more than just people your own age without children and pets: it was either Jewish people your own age without children and pets or Americans your own age without children and pets.

Back in the office, salesmen in all three alcoves were busy enticing visiting couples.

"No, I'm afraid we don't provide financing," one salesman was saying. "Of course, most people have cash from the sale of their homes."

"Yes, the monthly maintenance fee for the Timberline is an estimated hundred twenty-five dollars," another salesman was saying; "and that covers snow removal, water usage, trash collection, shuffleboard, landscaping, all clubhouse facilities, the roving security patrol, a twenty-four-hour nurse — everything, in fact, except golf."

"The Virginia Two and the Pennsylvania Two have walls attached," the third salesman was saying. "But you'll have no noise problem there."

It seemed to me, however, that the use of walls was really a frill, for I had heard no sound all morning but those Jewish church bells.

After a little more eavesdropping, I walked outside and stood for a couple of minutes on the lawn. People were slowly passing by, and most of them looked old to me: they walked slowly, their hair was either white or gone, and their faces were marked by the graffiti of time. Seeing them, I was struck by a disturbing truth about myself: I was a hypocrite who deplored the American worship of youth and yet was depressed by this wrinkled parade. Dr. Joyce Brothers kept saying that these people were not getting older, they were getting better; but this was the kind of doctor who inspired a second opinion. Once again, I had to make an effort not to shrink from these people who had earned the patronizing salute, "senior citizen." I wanted to work on this effort, however, with slightly *younger* older people.

An hour later I found my chance, a few miles down the road in a community called Concordia. The site of six hundred one-story homes built in 1981, Concordia courted what it called "the midlife market," a market I refused to admit I was part of: I was postponing my midlife crisis until I was sixty so I could live to a hundred and twenty.

After driving into Concordia and passing homes that sat back-to-back on the immaculately treeless streets, I reached a golf course where two couples were playing. I stopped my car near them, got out, and approached these two men and two women, none of whom looked more than sixty.

"Hi, I'm just browsing," I said, using an idiotic word for taking a look at golf. "How do you folks like it here?"

"We *love* it!" cried one of the women, who had just hit her putt as if she were playing for the Islanders. "It's like being at *camp*. Every day is Sunday!"

"Do you ever get tired of every day being Sunday?" I asked.

"Oh, no; this is *pre*retirement. The men go to work from here."

"We lived at Rossmoor for two years," said one of the men, "but this is better: a younger crowd."

My eye was distracted for a moment by a wooden swan on a nearby pond, while the other woman, in green shorts, pink lips, and blue veins, picked up the rhapsody with, "It's *heaven* here! I tell you, I'm afraid I'll wake up one day and something will happen to *change* it! When my husband got up this morning, I brought him right to the window. There was a mist coming off the pond with the artificial swan and I said, 'Doesn't that bring tears to your eyes?' "

I wondered if the mist had been artificial too, for there is little these communities do not arrange. Nevertheless, no matter how nature might have been rigged, these people had a heartening delight in life.

When I returned to my car, however, the radio assaulted me again with a less pleasant form of rejuvenation: "Chinese acupuncture *can* remove unwanted lines and wrinkles and make you feel younger!"

Damn! It was coming at me from all *sides!* Cover my spots and puncture my lines and color my hair and use *Family Circle*'s Anti-Aging Diet to chew my way to yesterday. The message never stopped: get *younger,* get *younger!* Tote that cream and lift that face! I'd been going in the wrong *direction* by awakening each morning one day older.

A few minutes later, I was in the men's locker room of the Concordia clubhouse, where a naked golfer in his late fifties was blotting a belly that belonged in a class on Lamaze. As exercise, golf was close to changing typewriter ribbons.

"I'm thinking of preretiring here," I told him. "I'm a writer, so I've had a lot of preretirement practice. You really like this place?"

"I sure do," he said. "When we came here, my wife thought she was at camp."

"Yes, I keep hearing that."

"It's *true:* on Labor Day, she felt like she had to go back home."

"Is there enough for you to do?" I said.

"Are you kidding? Golf, bowling, fishing, bridge — it's really *semi*retirement here."

"What's the difference between *semi*retirement and *pre?*"

"They're both terrific." He gestured to another nude of about his age standing nearby. "Harry here can't even find enough time for his model planes."

"And the women have enough to do?"

"Oh, sure," said Harry. "They even clean. You know women."

It was, of course, a sexist remark, and it made me aware that the adult community was a strange blend of America's future and America's past, of tomorrow's segregation and yesterday's ideas.

At the announcements board in the main lobby of the clubhouse, I saw all the busyness the golfer had meant: a great range of clubs, sports, and events, as well as a request from a woman for a female companion to drive to Palm Beach, and the offers of rental homes at Century Village in Boca Raton and at King's Point in Delray Beach. Century Village and King's Point were two of the places I planned to see. Was there operating in America a leisure village swap network for people who moved to another when they tired of one? People who scurried from one safe base to another like children playing tag? And if you slipped, you fell back into the world.

"I'm thinking of buying here," I told a man in madras shorts. "Either semiretirement or pre, whichever I can afford. I've just been to Rossmoor and Clearbrook."

"The houses are better here," he said. "At Rossmoor and Clearbrook they're built on slabs, but here there's crawl space underneath."

"You do much crawling under the house?" I asked him.

"No, I haven't been under yet."

"Why did you pick central Jersey for this kind of thing?"

"Well, I'm halfway between a grown son in Brooklyn and one in Baltimore," he said. "And this place has Mah-Jongg, ceramics, lectures — all that stuff."

"You like Mah-Jongg, ceramics, and lectures?"

"Can't stand 'em. But my wife does."

"So you moved here for *her?*"

"Well, I tell you, with a lot of couples, one likes it more than the other. But isn't that the way with every-thing in marriage?"

I was pondering his view of unsynchronized marriage when the siren of an ambulance suddenly sounded in a nearby street. Turning toward it, I said, "I suppose you hear that often."

"Enough," he said.

"Does it ever bother you?"

"You don't think about it. You just stay busy and think about the next day."

"Do you have a fixed routine?"

"No, it's quite fluid. One day I go to Spanish class, one day I bowl, and the rest of the time, whatever my wife has in mind. There's always something to do. Like the party at the Foodtown today."

"A supermarket right *here?*"

"Yeah, that's the party, the opening."

"There's none at Clearbrook."

"I told you, this is better."

When I left him, I walked down the main clubhouse hall, passing the art room, where two women in their sixties sat at tables working with clay. They *were* like children at camp, but campers who had stayed fifty years after the season.

Back in the sales office, I was shown a ten-minute film about Concordia. It was more than a cinematic salute to the place, it was an artistic attack on spontaneous living. After filling out a Prospective-Buyer Card, I went into a small screening room with a few other people and saw a production that began with a robust man in his fifties running down a leafy lane in a designer jogging suit. Suddenly, he stopped and asked me, "Aren't you sick of painting the house and doing the attic? Aren't you sick of pulling the weeds and mowing the lawn? Are you supposed to keep living in the old neighborhood just because you have a life sentence there?"

A female jogger in a matching suit now stopped beside him to pick up the theme.

"The neighborhood is *different* now," she said. "Our friends have moved and the kids grew older and left. So instead of driving them to tennis lessons, we've signed up for our own. Instead of PTA, we've signed up for gourmet."

Their argument made sense, but it still saddened me. *I've* loved *PTA meetings,* I thought. *Back-to-School Night is a Mardi Gras for me. And I've* loved *driving my three girls to their tennis lessons and their ballet lessons and the circus and — why, I've driven them to half of their* childhood.

These eager dropouts were resenting the kind of in-volvement with children that had been my greatest pleasure in life. I had always deplored such people, who couldn't wait for their children to finish growing up so a life without them could begin.

"Boy, was it great to get out from under that house," the male jogger said. "Sell high, buy low, and no more working for the landlord."

What did the landlord think, I wondered, *about your selling his house?*

"Now we have what we really need," said the woman. "Time, security, and privacy. A place where a concierge takes our packages *and* gets our theater tickets. For the first time in your life, you have *control* of your life. So have the *time* of your life. You've earned it!"

I was amused by the use of the word "concierge" in central New Jersey, a region more known for its cranberries than its crepes suzette. I was also amused when a woman who called herself Concordia Sales Consultant came up to me at the end of the film and said, "You know, we're also very close to all the wonderful things in Princeton."

"One of them is my wife," I replied. "That's where I live."

"Oh, it's *lovely* there, of course. But this is a different way of life. I think you should really see our models."

And so I did, discovering that the models at Concordia made Rossmoor and Clearbrook seem like urban renewal projects. A model called the Kingsley was $149,000, with a monthly community charge of $147.00, and another $18.41 a month if you wanted to use the sewer. Inside the Kingsley, a one-story house with two bedrooms, two bathrooms, and a two-car garage, I found a microwave oven, a lofted living-room ceiling, Yardley designer cabinets, a colonial six-panel closet, laminate counter tops with their own lighting, wall-to-wall carpeting in every room, and intrusion alarms on all windows and doors. And in a silver frame on the living-room table was a picture of a small blond boy, a generic grandchild. It made me think of the pictures of Gene Tierney that used to come with new wallets, a fitting thought in this house, for only people moving here would have known who Gene Tierney was. My legs were still too springy for this place where electric sockets were high on the walls so the residents did not have to bend.

As I stood in this gleaming modern home, dreamily letting the strains of "Laura" drift through my brain and bear me back to a senior prom on the Starlight Roof a few days before North Korea attacked, a woman with a leathery face walked in and told me that she and her husband were moving here from Brooklyn.

"You think you'll miss Brooklyn?" I asked her.

With a smile, she pointed toward an archway where her husband was coming through.

"*He* will," she whispered. "This was my idea."

Once again, a couple was dropping out not in sync.

"Brooklyn offers nothing if you don't have your family there," she said. "You know how it is with the family. You got memories, but nobody's around."

While she spoke about memory and desire, about losing kids but still wanting to be near them, I noticed a box on the wall with buttons and signs that made me think of the defense of North America:

CONCORDIA SECURITY

FIRE	READY
POLICE	ARMED
MEDICAL	A. C.

Perhaps her husband could learn to be happy in this benevolent bunker. Perhaps he would meet that other fellow who was also dragged here from Brooklyn, and then they could reminisce about Ebbets Field while hating lectures, ceramics, and Mah-Jongg.

About ten minutes later, when I left the house, a young woman in a tight T-shirt, who was taking care of some flowers, looked up and smiled at me; and in a sudden flight from staid security, from all the Concordian control, I walked over to this ripe gardener and began to feel a lovely desire to do some seeding of my own. I realized again that I spent ninety percent of my time thinking about sex and ninety percent thinking about age. This made a hundred eighty percent, of course, but I had always been an overachiever.

"Think you'd like to live here?" I asked the young woman, a less tired pass than *Don't I know you from the 4-H Club?*

"God, no," she replied. "*I* don't want everything done for me. But I guess that's what old people want. And another thing: I'd hate a place where everyone was *like* me."

"So where *would* you retire?"

"To a real *city*. With noise and dogs and kids — and even *dirt*."

Watching the scenic rise and fall of her chest, I wondered how many Concordians still wanted the one thing that the community couldn't supply. How sexual were these people in the privacy of their landscaped little police state? Now that they had endlessly uninterrupted time, did they remember the only improvised diversion left, the only one not listed on the big office sign that said

WHIRLPOOL

TENNIS

INDOOR POOL

BICYCLING PATHS

SHUFFLEBOARD COURTS

BILLIARD ROOM

PHOTO LAB

CRAFT ROOMS

LOUNGES

CARD ROOM

LIBRARY

PUTTING GREEN

EXERCISE ROOM

SAUNA

JOGGING PATHS

TV AND SOCIAL ROOMS

INVESTMENT SEMINARS

SHOWERS

"But not *all* old people want this, you know," I said to her. "There are people in my town — a lot of them *women* — in their seventies who ride bikes to the market and the library and do hard volunteer work too."

I turned for a moment and looked out at the golf course with its electric carts, seeing people who never biked to the market, just played it; and I remembered what Willie Keith's father had told him in *The Caine Mutiny:* Americans were soft on the outside, but they had a tough core.

But wasn't this the *time* to be soft? Retirement wasn't supposed to be the Battle of Midway.

"Yeah, I guess there's a few like that," the gardener said. "But this crowd, they're pampered like babies."

"It's not the real world, is it?" I said with the sociological acumen of Donald Duck.

"No, it's like a fantasy, like something for kids."

Her mention of kids reminded me of the mother of mine, so I ended this pleasant encounter and returned to the generation I was exploring. I walked back to the main office, where I wandered into a room that had a huge television screen, the Concordia Control Center, to which every home was wired for the instant detection of intruders, illness, or fire. And outside, enriching all this Orwellian delight, security guards were cruising the streets, past homes in which people needed permission to paint a single board.

"Hi!" said the hockey player I had met on the golf course. "Did you buy yet?"

"Not yet," I replied. "I'm still checking the figures on crime."

"Well, you'd better move *fast*. If you buy now, you'll still have to wait a year to get in; they're selling 'em like ice-cream cones."

"Listen," I said, "I'm a little confused: what are the management's rules about children? I know you can't give *birth,* but what else?"

"They're not the *management*'s rules: they're made by the Homeowners Association. Children are welcome, but most people would rather just see them on holidays."

And then she gave me a slightly suspicious look, as if wondering if *I* were a nonholiday child lover, and she

walked away. So it was just Christmas kisses and Cha-
nukah hugs for grandma here; but when I was a boy, my
grandmother had been in my home most of the time,
telling me stories, baking cakes, and playing piano ter-
ribly. She cared less for bridge with adults than for "London Bridge" with my sister and me; and so we grew up
among three generations, in a world where we were never
shunted about like rented cars.

My grandfather, who took me to ballgames and barber
shops, had been an even more enjoyable friend than my
grandmother. During our years together, he taught me
that the Giants would always break your heart by Labor
Day, that farmers fed eggshells back to chickens to help
them produce, and that Leslie Howard was Jewish, all
information that never made it to Trivial Pursuit. He was,
in fact, the proud scorekeeper of Zion, and the happiest
day of his life was either the day he got married or the
day I told *him* that Dinah Shore was Jewish.

"Dinah *Shore?*" he said with rising delight. "The *blond*
one with the *southern accent* . . . she's one of *my* kind?"

By "my kind" he didn't mean an unemployed florist:
he meant a famous person who surreptitiously was giving
him glory by passing as a Protestant. I collected many
things as a boy, from trolley transfers to baseball cards,
but nothing was more fun than helping my grandfather
build his collection of surprising Jews, that tinseled He-
braic underground whose infiltration of the establishment
allowed him to poke a passing Methodist and say, "You
know that Leslie Howard? The blond movie star with
the fancy accent and the ruler for a nose? Well, on Yom
Kippur, he doesn't act."

Now, however, that homey world in which grandfathers taught grandsons about swooning Giants, secret Jews, and chicken sex had been replaced by a world in which grandfathers talked about grandsons to other grandfathers in hiding with them. Such segregation at Clearbrook and Concordia seemed to be pleasing most of them; but still the nagging question remained: Did older Americans really *want* life to be sanitized and packaged for them like a glass in a motel room? Anthropologist Ashley Montagu had told me, "Most societies throughout history have preferred heterogeneity." Nevertheless, in spite of this timeless preference, the campers at Clearbrook and Concordia had chosen homogeneity and they seemed to like golf, ceramics, and bridge and even lectures on doom in the company of their own kind. Had they truly found the geriatric Good Life here? Or had they just been lured into becoming the lotus-eaters of today? I needed to leave New Jersey and see much more: I needed to look beyond pre and semiretirement. It was beyond *post*retirement that I didn't want to see.

As I walked back to my car, thoughts were filling my brain, where there was certainly room for them: dozens of Soviet Georgians worked hard, made love, did yogurt commercials, and lived with five generations when they were more than a hundred years old. . . . "The older I get, the luckier I am," Natalie Wood had said; and then, giving equal time to the opposite point of view, she had said, "I want yesterday." . . . "Go to a *retirement* community?" one of the seventy-year-old bicycling women in my town had said. "Can you imagine living in a place where you never hear a baby cry? No, I *like* all the ages and I *like* ups and downs." Maybe that was it, what was missing — contrast. Can there be ups if there are no downs?

And when would *Hugh* Downs stop telling me how great
it was to be eighty-three? . . . Of course, I *did* like the
headline in this week's *National Enquirer:* COUPLE, AGE 90,
EXPECT FIRST BABY. I needed to see more fathers like that
on Back-to-School Night.

I had barely left Concordia when the radio started playing "While We're Young" and I began to ache with longing for a time that now seemed like a dream, for a day
on my honeymoon in Paris, when I wasn't checking my
cheeks for new lines. Marilyn Monroe had done such
checking every morning. Clearly I was as crazy as she,
but this goddam awareness of age was what we *breathed*
in America; and even the radio's change to a traffic report
couldn't silence the lovely lyrics that were almost driving
me mad, the celebrations of that single word that sounded
day and night in my head: *Songs were made to sing while
we're young. . . . Now is the time for it, while we are
young. . . . Then younger than springtime am I . . . I'm gonna
wash that gray right out of my hair!*

Young, young, young. I had the mental balance of
Mighty Joe Young; but I did know that I wanted something more in a leisure village than these in central New
Jersey. It was time for me to go to the Sun Belt, and I
would begin with Florida. For years, my mother and
Judy's had been rhapsodizing about Florida, especially the
cheap dinners if you ate before six.

H. Irwin Levy
Had a Dream

PART II

B efore I could leave New Jersey for the Sun Belt, the Sun Belt came to me in the form of bagels and brochures from Century Village at the Treadway Inn in Saddle Brook, New Jersey. Of all the leisure villages in America, none recruited as rampantly as this south Florida chain begun in 1968 by a builder named H. Irwin Levy. Century Village snared you with full-page ads, with televised commercials, and with the kind of catered pressure that I was about to feel.

This has to be a classy operation, I thought as I entered the Treadway's parking lot. H. Irwin Levy has the ring of W. Somerset Maugham and G. Gordon Liddy.

Moreover, a brochure in my mail already had told me that Century Village, with forty thousand people in communities at West Palm Beach, Deerfield Beach, Boca Raton, and Pembroke Pines, considered itself not a leisure village but a *way of life,* like Buddhism or crime. Evangelical rallies like this one were being held every few months in

New York, New Jersey, and Connecticut; and every few weeks, a merry shill named Red Buttons, his beckoning arms held wide and a smile on his old baby face, told readers of huge newspaper ads to follow him to "that Red Buttons place, Century Village." Twenty years ago, when he was packing houses instead of selling them, Red Buttons used to chant, "Strange things are happening." And he still could be chanting it to describe the way that H. Irwin Levy has been skimming the generations from American life.

At 6:30 on a Thursday evening, I walked into the Treadway meeting room where three of Red's disciples were setting up their projector and charts. People in their late fifties, sixties, and early seventies were taking their places at ten tables that held bagels, Danish pastry, and buyer-profile cards. At my table, I sat down between a sad-faced man named Jules Steinman and a Clairol blond named Sue Rudin, who kept smiling weakly at me, as if sensing that a college tuition for Eve-Lynn made me a less likely candidate for Century Village than for a village in Peru.

"Your wife couldn't make it?" she said with nosy sympathy.

"We couldn't get a sitter," I told her.

"You have young *children?*"

"Just one: she's eight."

"You can't bring her *with* you, you know."

"Oh, I know; we're just looking ahead — though she *is* quite mature."

"A woman at *one* of the communities — I forget which one — accidentally got pregnant and now they're trying to evict her. It's a big lawsuit because of the contract everyone signs. You have to agree you won't have children."

"They should keep her and sell *tickets,*" I said. "It sounds like the first miracle since Lourdes."

"No, she's just in her forties; they're trying to bring more young people in."

"By the time you're ready for this place," said Jules Steinman, "there'll be a Century Village at Tallahassee. Everything's moving north because of the Hispanics."

"Yes, even *Pompano* is borderline now," said Sue Rudin's husband, Sid. "The Hispanics keep moving up."

"But we can still counterattack," I said, feeling like General Grant. "We got Columbus Avenue back from them."

"It's really disturbing, that element," said a chubby woman named Joan Krantz with two-toned hair, some of which matched the cheese Danish. She was a woman of no more than fifty, who sat here alone with no wedding ring. I wondered why she was considering an adult community, where finding a husband seemed like the equivalent of a singles weekend in the Vatican. At Clearbrook, about twenty percent of the residents were widows, but the widowers were very few.

While a waitress filled our coffee cups, the conversation ranged over various aspects of Florida life in the Century Village sanctuaries:

"The best apartments at Boca are the two bedrooms for seventy-five thousand. . . . My aunt hated being a golf widow. The golfers and their wives live separate lives. . . . Anyone here ever been to the West Coast? . . . You think the Hispanics will go west too? . . . God, if I could just never see snow again. . . . But the doctors stink. They figure it's probably fatal, so what's the point? . . . I tell you, it's the Garden of Eden. . . . Some people are moving back. . . . It's paradise. . . . But you gotta take trips. You gotta have something to talk about besides health and wealth. . . . Don't forget the grand-children. . . . There's probably more for the Hispanics in the East, don't you think?"

"There's no *question* that places like Century Village are the answer for us," said Sid. "When your children are gone, it can get awful lonely in Nutley, New Jersey — which was never a jubilee to begin with. So what're you gonna do? Take in boarders? The old house is just too big and expensive to keep up, and half your crowd has already gone south. At a place like Century Village, you can start a whole new life with people just like us."

"That's the reason not to go," said Joan, and a few people laughed, but I sensed she was serious.

"I guess it *is* a second chance," I said to Sid.

"Absolutely. In a warm place, with no house to keep fixing and with ten thousand activities. Where you can finally do all the things you always *wanted* to do but were just too busy or too scared. You see, it's a lot *more* than being able to swim and play golf in December. It's a chance to start making *pottery* or making *jewelry* —"

"Or mud pies," said Joan.

At seven o'clock, Shirley Gray, a plump woman in her early fifties who was the Public Relations Director of Century Village, stepped to the microphone at the front of the room to introduce herself and John DeLuca, Vice President for Sales of Cenvill Corporation. And then, with the cheerful solemnity of someone who was spread-

ing The Word, Shirley Gray let us know that Martin
Luther King was not the only one to have a dream.

"H. Irwin Levy had a dream," she said.

A dream of mass relocation.

For the next ten minutes, she told us how he already
had led forty thousand people to the palmy promised
land: with 7,500 condominiums built in 1968 at the first
Century Village in West Palm Beach; with 8,500 condominiums built in 1971 at the second Century Village
in Deerfield Beach; with 5,780 condominiums built in
1979 at the third Century Village in Boca Raton; and with
7,750 condominiums built in 1984 at the fourth Century
Village in Pembroke Pines, 1,050 of which were sold and
the rest of which were going fast.

"Don't worry," Jules whispered to me, "there are plenty
of resales."

If money was a problem for you, seventy-five percent
of the price of your apartment could be financed by
H. Irwin Levy's own mortgage company; and while you
were writing your check, you could be watching a program on H. Irwin Levy's own cable television service;
but your stamp would have to come from the post office.
Century Village was still behind Albania and Paraguay.

Albania and Paraguay, however, had no apartments
connected to a computer that contained the medical history of every resident. When I heard Shirley say this, I
momentarily pictured my life with Judy in a home that
had electronic omniscience: a video screen above our stove
saying TOO MUCH CHOLESTEROL THIS WEEK, and another
above our bed saying WAIT! YOU FORGOT YOUR DIA-
PHRAGM.

". . . so you're buying more than *four walls*," Shirley said as she finished. "You're buying a *way of life*."

In the film that followed her talk, Red Buttons gave a performance that fell somewhere between his Academy Award role in *Sayonara* and a dramatic reading by Crazy Eddie.

"Remember how it used to be before life got serious?" Red said as the screen flashed shots of America at play in the 1920s, sweet memories for anyone eighty years old. "Well, it's time to put on those tennis, golf, and dancing shoes again. It's time to fall in love with *life* again!"

The screen now dissolved to Century Village, while Red got a bit misty himself. ". . . lush nature walks and jogging trails. . . . Congenial and accomplished neighbors from all walks of life. . . . Adults in the prime of life finding a new kind of freedom. . . . Pembroke Pines . . . giving you the best of today with the loveliest of yesterday and the finest of tomorrow."

After a few more quick alluring shots of Pembroke Pines, H. Irwin Levy, the old dreamer himself, came to the screen to extol his new "seven hundred twenty-four acre lakefront community in one of south Florida's most prestigious areas." In other words, a place south of the rednecks, east of the Seminoles, and north of the Cubans. And then, to counterbalance Levy's frankly sentimental view of Pembroke Pines, the film presented some man-in-the-street interviews.

"Living in Century Village is a *dream*," said a white-haired woman with a Bronx accent, who seemed to be in her middle sixties. "I wish I'd retired sooner. It's added fifteen years to my life!"

I began to wonder if there was a difference in average

life span between the Bronx and Boca Raton. Did endless leisure really extend it? I thought again of the Soviet Georgians, one of whom, at the age of one hundred and twelve, had told a gerontologist, "I love work like I love the air of our mountains. I always work — at the mill or as a shepherd. That is the secret of long life: work."

If playing bridge every day had added fifteen years to *her* life, then playing with sheep had added fifty to *his* — and there was no monthly charge for the maintenance of his mountain. Therefore, who had The Answer: Red Buttons or Red shepherds?

". . . so come on *down*," said a paunchy man in a bathing suit.

Come on down: the price was right: a two-bedroom, two-bathroom apartment in the Kingsley section could be mine for only thirty-seven thousand dollars, although one for sixty-five might add even *more* years to my life. The film was over now and the enticing statistics were coming live from John DeLuca, a young man with a dark mustache and a view of the future to match.

"By 1990," he said, "eighty-five percent of everything built in Florida will be a condominium."

This vision so depressed me — I saw bulldozers pushing all the alligators and Indians into Alabama — that I felt no lift when DeLuca made the Village's Fly-and-Buy offer to us:

"Spend three sun-filled days and two fun-filled nights as our guest. And then, when you buy, four hundred dollars in travel expenses will be repaid to you at closing."

He ended the evening with a few more words about his paved new world, but I was hearing Holden Caulfield saying, *Certain things they should stay the way they are.*

The following morning, I tossed the Fly-and-Buy pamphlet into a box beside my desk. On this desk was a mortgage book with monthly payments of $1,080. And suddenly, these payments felt more oppressive than they ever had; and just as oppressive felt the maintenance of this house that I performed with a blend of reluctance and ineptitude. If Judy and I lived at Clearbrook, Concordia, or Century Village, I would never have to mow the lawn, as I did now on national holidays; and I would never have to bear the ill will of my neighbors, who now felt they were living in the bush. I would never again have to clean out a roof gutter or spray a birch tree or use a sump pump to drain a basement that had become a reservoir. God and Guardian Development would handle it all.

After putting away the Fly-and-Buy pamphlet, I turned back to the present and plunged with all my strength into a sporting day with a contemporary of mine named Lori. We went to Princeton's public pool to swim in a father-daughter relay race, for last night's look at that Red Buttons place had left me even more determined to take the advice of Bob Dylan and stay forever young.

"Okay, honey," I told Lori as she took her mark to swim the first lap against four other girls. "Just bring me a twenty-yard lead and we'll win!"

A couple of the other fathers looked as though they could have been my sons; I was in a sporting version of *All My Children;* but intergenerational living had a new appeal for me. And so, after swimming our hearts out, Lori and I were able to finish fifth.

"It's not the score that counts," I said to her as we dried off. "It's how you play the game."

"And we played rotten," she said.

"But we'll come back next summer, honey, when all those other fathers are a year older."

She smiled, seeming to know that next summer I would still be just the same age. However, time's wingèd chariot began to overtake me again moments after we had returned to the house: the telephone rang and a strange voice said, "Mr. Schoenstein, this is Manny Frank of Century Village. You came to our dinner last night."

"Well, not really a *dinner*," I said. "All I got was Danish."

"Do you have any plans for coming down to Pembroke Pines?"

"Oh, certainly . . . maybe . . . sometime."

"You get two free days and three free nights, you know."

"Yes, I know."

"So whenever you're ready to come, just call me and we'll pick you up at the airport."

It was a pickup that I knew I could not avoid; but first I picked up Lori and took her into my bedroom for a game that we called "garbage": I pretended she was garbage and kept tossing her onto the bed, after which the wind blew her back to me and I sent the laughing trash flying again.

Coming into the bedroom, Judy watched our game of garbage for a while and then smiled sweetly at me and said, "I think they should recycle *you*."

"I'm just retreating from Century Village," I said. "I'm not going gentle into that good night."

My retreat, however, was brief, for five days later I landed at Fort Lauderdale and was met by the Century

Village van. The air was like a sauna, one of the features of Florida not captured by H. Irwin Levy or Red.

"Is it always this *steamy?*" I asked the driver as we headed for the Holiday Inn at Calder.

"Only half the year," he said. "But you got central air conditioning at all the Villages. You don't have to breathe much of this."

"What do you think of the Villages?" I said, guessing that he didn't live in one because he looked twenty-five.

"They're okay, I guess. Everything's becoming a mall, so why not a mall for old people where they won't get mugged?"

"Like a Sears full of seniors."

"Yeah, they paid their dues."

"But the thing is, no country has *ever* had whole cities with just elderly people. I mean, never in the history of *civilization* have older people gone into exile in such numbers."

"No shit," he said, happy to be enlightened by my Cliff Notes sociology; but then a quiet thoughtfulness came over us both and we rode in silence through the muggy Florida flatness to the Holiday Inn, where I continued my colloquy with a maid of more than sixty, who had not finished making up my room.

"Go to a place like *that?*" she said. "And live with all those *old* people? That's no good for anyone. Where ya goin' — Pembroke, West Palm, or Boca?"

"I'm not sure," I said. "Which one swings?"

"Well, forget West Palm; they're half dead there. Boca's got a lotta Hungarians, if that's what ya like."

Part Hungarian myself, I felt that my kinsmen would bring a certain élan to even the dullest place; and so, after another promotional dinner, I picked up my brochures and started north in a van with a dozen other Fly-and-Buyers and a Century Village flack named Rose Tannenbaum. I now had one of the world's biggest private collections of Century Village brochures, all of which said

Sleep tight security. What a beautiful way of life.

"I'm just wondering if there'll be enough for my mother to *do,*" said a man in his thirties, who sat between his mother and me.

"Enough to *do?*" said Rose Tannenbaum. "You have nothing to do but fill your days with activities!"

You have nothing to do but fill your days with activities. The words lingered with me as we moved up Interstate 95, past billboards that said

The Feeling of Security Is All Around
When You Live at Century Village

". . . it's twenty-eight thousand for the lowest floor of a three-story building with a twelve-year mortgage," Rose Tannenbaum was saying to a short chubby man who wore a Hebrew letter on a gold chain.

"You don't have to sell me," he said. "I know what these houses would cost outside. But that's not the big reason we're coming. The big reason is our children treat us lousy now and we're —"

"Harry, for God's *sake!*" said a woman beside him. "You're the ten o'clock news?"

"*I'm* not ashamed, *they* should be. One quick Sunday call and *never* anything else. They don't live fifty miles away and always too busy to see us."

"Harry!"

"I'm sure we're not the only ones. Maybe down here we'll find some people whose kids *also* treat 'em lousy. I mean, it's something in common, right?"

As we approached Boca Raton, Rose and the others continued to talk, but I was hearing the new weekly call that would be coming to Harry and his wife, a generic call in America today, the Sunday Morning Sun Belt Connection:

"Hello, Mom."

"Well, I've been wondering *when we'd hear from you, stranger."*

"Mom, I'm not a stranger. I'm your son Sam and we talked last Sunday. We talk every *Sunday."*

"And that's so hard?"

"Of course *it's not so hard."*

"The Kleins' son calls twice a week."

"Here we go with the Bell Olympics. Who else *am I competing with?"*

"Drop that tone; I just meant they seem to hear so much more about their grandchildren than your father and I do."

"Jesus, it's not a goddam contest. *Beat the Grandmothers."*

"Is that talk necessary, Sam? Do you have to bring Jesus into this?"

"Mom, let's start again. Hello, how's the weather there?"

"All right, I guess."

"What do you mean you 'guess?' Don't you look *at it?"*

"It's been a little cold for swimming."

"But you don't swim anyway."

"It's nice to have you call me to argue."

"Artie just got back from Palm Beach and he says the weather's been fine."

"*You're Mister District Attorney now? Maybe if you'd gone to law school instead of just teaching English . . .*"

"*Are you and Dad feeling okay?*"

"*We're still alive, if anyone cares.*"

"*Now what the hell is* that *supposed to mean? You have a gorgeous place in Century Village and all you do is complain. What have you been* doing *with yourselves all week?*"

"*We try to keep busy.*"

"*Look, I know it's hard to do nothing, but you really have to —*"

"*Who says we do nothing? This place has everything —* you *know that.*"

"*What about the volunteer work I mentioned? Reading to kids at the hospital?*"

"*You know the kind of* people *they get at the hospital?*"

"*You mean* sick *people?*"

"*Don't be smart with me, Sam. If you're so smart, why can't you send us to Europe like the Frankels' son?*"

"*Now it's the Travel Ticket Olympics.*"

"*We never hear from the children. They never write.*"

"*It's the Information Age; who writes? Mom, I didn't tell you to move away from the real world.*"

"*You* know *the winters in Yonkers.*"

"*Yeah, Tolstoy wrote about them.*"

"*More smartness.*"

"*I wish you were still in a place where you could see the leaves turn.*"

"*Why don't you all come down for a while? All the Herberts just came down and the Kramer kids have been here for a week.*"

"*Mom,* please *don't give me the Eastern Airlines scorecard.*"

"*Well, you're all strangers to me.*"

"*Go on, I bet you could pick us out in a lineup.*"

"*I'm supposed to laugh?*"

"*Once in a while, yes. You're living in a paradise and you never laugh.*"

Our van reached the Boca Raton gatehouse a few minutes after six, and we entered the place where ten thousand exiles already lived. In all directions, three- and four-story white buildings rose severely above sterile streets, making the area seem to me like East Berlin with palms. After the van had parked inside the gate, Rose led us to Check Point Two at the entrance to the big colonial-style clubhouse, where two more guards admitted us to an enormous main floor full of people in their sixties and seventies, most of whom were sitting impassively. I could find nobody smiling. The room had the joie de vivre of a sperm bank.

As Rose led us through, she said, "You know, the Century Village way of life has grown so popular that people in their fifties and even *forties* are buying at Pembroke Pines. We have five thousand on the waiting list."

I was fifty-one, but I felt like an impostor. Fifty-one was my *father's* age.

And now she led us down a long hall, while Muzak piped out the soft mockery of "The Way We Were." Passing one room, I heard other music and saw a flabby woman waltzing about the floor alone, like a gelatinous Zelda Fitzgerald.

"These are multipurpose rooms," said Rose. "They can be used for classes or lectures or anything else."

"Like movies?" I said.

"No, movies are in the auditorium. In fact, tonight we

son is angry because they moved here and they're angry at him for being angry."

"It's nice when people have something in common."

"They'll probably leave their money to cats."

When it was time for me to leave Eva and return to the tour, I impulsively kissed her on the cheek.

"You'll make some woman a nice husband," she said.

"My wife says it's always possible. Look, I really hope . . . well, that maybe you'll find someone."

"I probably wouldn't marry him. Just live with him like most of the others. The Social Security, you know."

"Yes, I know. Moonlight and Medicare."

A few minutes later, I was back with the tour as it entered the auditorium, where about a hundred people were waiting for this week's culture movie. Before it began, a woman in her twenties came out on stage and said, "I have some important announcements. . . . First, tomorrow afternoon, there'll be registration for the defensive driving course. That's *so* important, isn't it? . . . And on Thursday, there'll be a dance in honor of Sandra and Max. Now *that* really sounds like fun!"

Her tone was that of a kindergarten teacher announcing the arrival of a new rabbit; but it was the official tone of the young addressing the old in America, where Helen Hayes traveled the land deploring those who kept saying, "I *like* old people."

The movie was as patronizing as the young woman: a life of Mozart made in Germany for village idiots everywhere. In one unforgettable scene, a happy-go-lucky Beethoven came to Mozart's house and said, "Good morning, Mr. Mozart. Would you like to hear me play the piano?"

Suddenly fearing that I was about to hear Mr. Mozart say to Mr. Salieri, "Hey, *I* know what we'll do! Let's put on a *show!*" I walked out of the auditorium. A few feet away, I found a small room with an upright piano, where I sat down and began to play "I'll Be Seeing You" in the dreamy and draggy style that had been the coup de grace at so many of my parties. Judy had said that everything I played sounded like "Auld Lang Syne," but she was wrong: my "Auld Lang Syne" didn't sound like "Auld Lang Syne." Nevertheless, in spite of my heartfelt search for the right notes, I played on, trying to send myself away from Century Village to the golden Manhattan where I'd been a boy.

"You play good," a voice behind me said, and I turned to see a man with curly white hair and a warm craggy face. His accent was either Russian or Polish and he clearly knew nothing about music.

"Thanks," I said as he sat down beside the piano, "but I really don't."

And then I saw it: the long blue number on his thickly muscled arm.

"You should go to the movie and hear Mozart play," I told him.

"They wouldn't let me in," he said. "I didn't have no ticket. *You* play like Mozart. Play Mozart for me."

"I . . . well, I'll try." And I wondered if he would believe that Mozart had written "Bye Bye Baby."

He was smiling now with half-closed eyes, while I was trying to transcend my lack of talent to entertain this survivor, who had slipped through a hole in the total entertainment package of Century Village. It was a moment of bittersweet absurdity, my almost making music

for this lost man; but I kept on playing, the way that
Mozart must have played at the age of seven months,
while my mind was hearing Red Buttons say, *Congenial
and accomplished neighbors . . . adults in the prime of life,
finding a new kind of freedom.*

In spite of his age and bewilderment, this man beside
me still looked so strong: his muscular arms made me
think of Al Oerter, the four-time Olympic discus champion, who had tried a fifth time to make the Olympics
at the age of forty-seven, and who then had said, "I'm
going to make a lousy old person."

Me too, Al, I thought. *Everyone* should try to make a
lousy old person, to echo Shakespeare's *Age, I do abhor
thee.*

"You know any Beethoven?" my listener asked.

"Just what he wrote for the Follies," I replied.

"Jan!" cried a voice behind us. "I've been looking all
over for you!" I turned to see a tall woman in a sweatsuit
coming into the room. She seemed in her mid-sixties,
with large alert eyes that were now regarding me. "And
who are *you?*"

"He's my Mozart," said Jan.

"Only my income is Mozart's," I told her. "I've come
down from New Jersey. I'm thinking of moving here."

"You'll love it."

"Well . . . I don't know. I've run into some melancholy people tonight."

"I can't imagine who they are," she said sharply. "All
the people *I* know are happy here. Every recreation
under the sun and lots of friends your own age who
remember the things you remember."

"Yes, but —"

"And no snow to shovel, and nobody's hitting you over the head, and *you* know any apartment for thirty-five thousand with no maintenance to do?"

"Hey, don't shoot the piano player. I know what you're saying. But I *have* met a couple of people who couldn't exactly be called happy."

"Of *course*, there's complainers everywhere. Like the one that got pregnant."

"Someone *here* got pregnant?" I said, wondering if this was the case I had heard about at Saddle Brook.

"Yes, someone who obviously didn't mind breaking the rules about children. She's around forty; her husband's older. And to make it worse, they're fighting eviction."

Before taking Jan away, this prickly friend of his told me the basis for the battle now in court: the unexpectant mother, upon choosing Century Village, had signed the standard buyer's contract saying there would be no children. And even children not newborn found no warm welcome here: those under eighteen visiting grandparents were allowed to use the pool, but none of the facilities in the clubhouse nor the golf course. A tot who shot a good game of pool had to settle for watching Willie Mosconi on ABC.

"Good-bye, Mozart," said Jan as he left.

"Good-bye, Jan. I loved playing for you."

When they had gone, I remained at the keyboard, no longer wondering about the right notes but now thinking of Jan's loneliness and of what the Beatles had called "all the lonely people." One of them could be *me*. What if Judy or I had to come to a leisure village to start a new life alone? Suddenly, I felt compelled to find out more about fresh starts.

If every day was Sunday, then every night was Saturday night, especially when Saturday really came. On the next legitimate Saturday night, I put on my dancing shoes, which I last had worn the week of the Bay of Pigs, and at eight o'clock I walked alone into the Grand Ballroom of the main clubhouse at Kings Point, a sprawling leisure village at Delray Beach. This was Cabaret Night, the weekly dance, and I was here to imagine the unthinkable: how I would feel to be sixty-five or seventy, without Judy, and trying to fall in love again.

Coming into this huge ballroom now was a mix of couples and singles, men and women in multicolored shirts, slacks, blouses, and dresses, who were starting to dance a variety of steps to a ballad played by a five-piece orchestra of residents up on the stage. Called the Kings Pointers, they were a CPA on horn, a dentist on sax, a dermatologist on guitar, a beautician on bass, and a gym teacher on drums. While the people entering presented tickets they had bought for $1.75, each of which held a seat at a table, the Kings Pointers played "The Second Time Around," the alma mater for many here. Outnumbering the single men by twenty-to-one, the single women here were optimists to equal the ancient Egyptians, who put boats in their tombs for afterlife cruises. In spite of the odds against their making connections, some of these optimists were already orbiting the floor, where mostly marrieds were slow-dancing beneath a crystal chandelier. Surrounding the dance floor, on a red carpet, were circular tables for ten to which people were bringing their own bottles, for no liquor was served on Cabaret Night. Only soft drinks and setups were there for both the nostalgic and the hopeful.

Standing now against a high wall that held golden sconces, I began to watch the dancers, wondering if the married ones were trying to recapture a magic that perhaps they'd never had.

"Do you come here often?" I suddenly found myself asking a woman with half-blond hair, whose flowered blouse hung over red pants. And then I remembered that this was the very line I had used for seduction in my teens. At least I hadn't asked what her major was.

"Sometimes," she replied with a sweet little smile.

"My name is Ralph Schoenstein."

"Pleased to meet you. I'm Ella Klein."

"Are you . . . alone?"

"A widow. I'm alone at these things too. In three years, I've met maybe one and a half men."

"The odds are tough for a woman, I see."

"Oh, it *can* happen; we have weddings here. And some just move in together. I'm in a singles club. A new man joined a few months ago and he got snatched up before I could even find out his name. Anyhow, I'm not really sure I want it. The men only marry 'cause they need someone to cook and clean and give sex. Let them hire a maid."

"Who's also a prostitute. Or else a prostitute who cleans."

"Yes," she said, smiling again, "that's what they need."

"Would you like to dance?" I said as the music changed to "Sunrise, Sunset."

"Oh, that's nice; you don't have to."

"When you see how I dance, you won't think it's so nice."

"Don't feel you gotta be a social worker. I just like to come here and listen to the music."

But *I* didn't like listening to this particular music because "Where is the little girl I carried?" made my heart sink. In fact, this song sent me reeling in all directions through time: Lori growing up and Judy possibly coming to a dance like this alone and myself back at a Stuyvesant High School prom, holding Sandra Kramer's hand with a palm so sweaty that I almost watered her wrist corsage.

My dancing partner thirty-five years after dampening Sandra was a woman of sixty-five, whose husband had sold dresses in New York. I was moving her slowly around a floor on which fifty people were dancing when I said, "I have to tell you: I'm married."

"The shock doesn't kill me," she said. "By the way, that's more than some of them say."

"Do you ever get a chance to meet any . . . possible single men?"

"Just impossible ones. All the girls, they want a rich one, but me. . . . Look, I'm living on borrowed time."

"Sixty-five isn't old."

"If you're eighty."

"Where do you meet men — besides these dances?"

"Here and there. Even in the supermarket parking lot. But such *shlemiels*. I cooked a dinner for one and he fell asleep over it. And another one I cooked for, he tried to take me to bed before we ate. Next time I'll serve tuna fish."

For another minute we danced silently while I pondered the melancholy business of starting again, the endless indignities a woman like this had to bear. When the music changed to a lumbering version of "Tico, Tico," I said, "This is a samba, Ella. I'm afraid I've never learned it.

Of course, the band hasn't either and they're still going on."

"Come, we'll sit down and have a ginger ale," she said. "I'm at table six."

"Yes, that would be nice."

Together we crossed the floor to her table, where another woman with half-blond hair was removing a sandwich from her handbag. Seeing me, she sheepishly said, "They don't sell it here."

Ella and I sat down with her and a deeply tanned man of about seventy, who was one of the few men in a sports jacket.

"Ella, good to see you, sweetheart," he said. "Any action yet?"

"Sy, you *know* I just come for the music," she replied.

"Well, I'll check around and see if anyone's wife is terminal."

Ella broke the uneasy silence that followed this tasteless joke by introducing me. Sy, who was a lawyer, then began to entertain us with talk about his IRA account, but the band did better: it hit a fanfare and the guitarist stepped forward and cried, "Okay, everybody, *singles* line! Guys over here, gals over there. Then let's pair off and *dance!*"

As the band started playing "People" and the singles formed their lines on both sides of the floor, Sy said, "Okay, Ella, go get 'em!"

"*Please,*" she said with a look at a scene that was not quite the ball of the Capulets. "Let me skip the meat market."

"Ralph," said Sy, "what about *you?*"

"I'm a vegetarian too," I told him; but then I saw that

the male line was much shorter than the female one, an offense to my sense of symmetry that moved me to add my modest weight to the men.

As the lines began coming together, I remembered such lines at high school dances, when this was a giddy game and not a desperate one. While the band stayed with "People," the players in this romantic roulette kept pairing off until I met my partner at last: a dark-haired woman of indeterminate age, with drum-tight skin that glistened with makeup, a bosom uncontainable by a low-cut dress, and the kind of hips that were popular in Argentina. I was flushed with my luck at being able to leave social work to dance with a swinger.

"Do you come here?" I said, speaking almost all of my timeless opening as we started to dance.

"Do I *come* here?" she said. "Whadda ya mean? I'm *here*."

"*Often,* I mean; often — and it doesn't matter; I'm Ralph Schoenstein."

"Hi, I'm Gloria Piano. Don't tell me *you* live here."

"No, but I'm thinking of coming."

"Alone?"

"Well, no; I'm married — and she feels well." I smiled and she did too.

"You're cute," she said. "Even if you *are* on a singles line."

"I'm sorry. I know it's unfair to widows for me. . . ."

"I'm divorced. I didn't kill him like most of the others."

"Have you been here long?"

"Too long. I need a younger place. So do you."

Because there was no future for her in dancing with me, I felt guilty about wasting her time, and time was no small concern for her: a close look at her face revealed that she was probably in her middle or late sixties like most of the rest: plastic surgery had been her transportation to a better decade. Her too-tight skin, however, mocked my own ludicrous yearning to be Dorian Gray.

We spoke little for the rest of "People," but then the music changed to what was either a rhumba or a march and I said, "Want to sit down awhile?"

"No, I like to keep moving," she said. "Thanks for the dance." And her hips, which had always been her own, twisted into the crowd.

Returning to Ella's table, I found it full of people, one of whom, a small bald man, was telling his wife, "By five *minutes* we missed it and the steak went up three bucks. You dress so damn *slow*."

"You eat so damn cheap," she replied.

They were discussing Florida's legendary Early Bird dinners, whose prices remained low until six o'clock.

"It's a crime to pay those regular prices."

"Harry, how many times must I tell you: I'm not *hungry* at five-thirty. That's for children and hospitals."

"Okay, we'll move lunch up to eleven-thirty."

"And breakfast to seven, which would be intravenous 'cause you're still asleep."

"Come on, Ella, we'll try one more," I said, leading her back to the floor. "I'm not sure what they're playing, but it's better than that argument."

"The Early Bird is the big thing down here," she said. "But not for me: I don't date men who run for matinee prices. I don't need gypsy violins, but I do like the sun to be down."

A few minutes later, when the music stopped, I took

Ella back to the table, and then I said good-bye. The dance would be ending at eleven so the minibuses could take the people back to their apartments, but I had already stayed at the party too long. Why take a chance on breaking the heart of some other woman who was seeking an unmarried prince to take her to dinner at six-fifteen?

Walking away from the clubhouse, I heard "Saturday Night Is the Loneliest Night of the Week," but in my own head. Gloria had been right: I needed a younger place, one with more freedom, vitality, and cheer. It was time to go West, middle-aged man.

On the Banks
of Sun City

PART III

In the beginning, there was Sun City, the first leisure village since Sodom, and one with similar weather. Built just northwest of Phoenix, Arizona, in 1960, Sun City eventually grew to 25,000 people, the size of my hometown of Princeton; and then, in 1978, it spawned Sun City West, which became the fastest growing adult community in America. And it was to these quietly booming twin cities, this mother lode of leisure, that I came on a cloudless Sunday morning in October. I came with Judy, Lori, and a Cabbage Patch Kid named Mindy, my trendy "granddaughter," who made me feel that the years were passing even faster than they were.

At Sun City's Kings Inn Motel, where a bumper sticker said SUPPORT BINGO — KEEP GRANDMA OFF THE STREET, I felt like a Moslem entering Mecca. Century Village, Rossmoor, Clearbrook, Concordia, and a thousand other leisure worlds would not have been born had it not been for a builder named Del Webb, who claimed the Southwest for seniors as boldly as Coronado had claimed it for Spain.

In the Kings Inn coffee shop, where I took a table with Judy, Lori, and Mindy, I was surrounded by people who must have known Coronado. After one man in a string tie and cowboy hat had finished a five-minute walk across the room, Judy said, "I hope we can walk like that when we're his age."

"I think I miss the sparkle of Century Village," I replied.

This was the deepest immersion into age I had made, and the discomfort I felt made me wonder if those who had fled the intergenerational life knew something that I was too dumb or dishonest to admit. Shakespeare, who knew everything, had looked at such decline and despaired with the words, "When I have seen by Time's fell hand defaced . . ." Would I *ever* be able to accept the defacement as God's graffiti? Time's fell hand was why I had brought Lori with me, depriving her of two weeks of the third grade, when she would have learned to spell elephant. She was growing up too fast and I still had found no way to freeze each precious age; I simply had to keep savoring and remembering the moments. With all three daughters, in fact, I had often been guilty of premature nostalgia, of reminiscing about sweet times while they were going on. By constantly looking back at the present, I had given new meaning to relativity.

After breakfast, I took Lori to the shuffleboard court, where her loud merry voice kept piercing the still air and jarring the people who were dormant nearby. Did she represent to these sleepwalkers something they wanted to forget? Or did she represent a profound lack in their lives, one discussed by a spunky woman of ninety-two in *The View in Winter,* who said, "Don't go to those dreadful old folks' clubs, but find some young people. Put up with their casualness because it's worth it."

I wanted to play with Lori all day, but it was time to leave her now and explore this mother lode, which a motel clerk had told me was anything but dreadful. After setting up Judy and Lori at the pool, and making sure that Mindy wouldn't get too much sun, I got into my car and drove down Del Webb Boulevard, soon passing a billboard that said

DEL WEBB'S INCOMPARABLE
SUN CITY WEST

It was just ten in the morning, but a sign on the Valley National Bank told me that the temperature already was 82. And then, on the car radio, a woman said to me, "My husband Carl has given me many things in our thirty-three happy years, but nothing to compare with our move to Leisure World at Mesa." She rhapsodized for another minute about her new home, and then she said, "Every time I pass the friendly guard, I realize it was love at first sight — with Carl and Leisure World."

What a prince, that Carl, taking his sweetheart out of circulation so tenderly. There was, however, no friendly guard at Sun City West, and no barbed wire or gate of any kind, for this was an open community, old enough to feel secure. As I drove down the wide main street, I passed endless one-story houses, some set against cacti and palms, and then I passed two shopping malls. Unlike Century Village and Concordia, Sun City West was a self-contained community: it was possible to live here and never have to leave for supplies; and you also were nestled against your money, for one short section of this street contained *eight banks*. There was, therefore, a bank for every fourteen hundred people, and I wondered how all of them could survive. Something was going on here that went beyond toasters for new accounts; but this was Sunday and I would have to wait until tomorrow to learn the secret of the bonnie bonnie banks of Sun City West.

Turning into the R. F. Johnson Recreation Center, I parked in front of West Hall and wandered into the Covenant Presbyterian Church, where an organ was playing "Jesu, Joy of Man's Desiring," a song that I was able to play so it sounded like "You Took Advantage of Me."

"Welcome!" said a woman with hymnals at the rear of the hall. "We're happy to have you worship with us."

"Thanks," I said, "but I'm just passing through. And I'm Jewish."

"Oh, that doesn't make any difference."

No wonder the Presbyterian Church lacked the Catholic clout: visiting bar-mitzvah boys were embraced. I did, however, know the doxology from having attended compulsory chapel at Hamilton College; but it had been thirty-four years since I had raised my heathen voice to praise Father, Son, and Holy Ghost.

As I took a seat in the last row of the white-headed congregation, I thought about Hamilton, not only because of that tainted doxology but also because a young graduate named Jennifer Rubin had recently been murdered by people she was helping in the Peace Corps in Togo. Since Father, Son, and Holy Ghost had allowed such an awful absurdity, I wondered for the thousandth time if it made any difference whether people spent Sun-

day morning here with their Good Books or with their
bankbooks at home. Some dividends were clearly more
certain than others; and it was the uncertain ones that had
moved me to write my own agnostic's prayer:

> *Dear God, who may not exist, guide me*
> *through the madness, for sanity's sake.*

I slipped this prayer into the service; and a few minutes
later, I slipped out of the hall and ecumenically entered
the Lutheran Coffee Hour in the building next door. The
wandering Jew was more comfortable here, and soon I
was talking to a man in a green sports jacket, whose voice
was rampantly hearty and whose smile was working too
hard. I kept expecting him to show me the new Chev-
rolets.

"I'm not a Lutheran, I'm a writer," I said, aware that
my disclaimer still needed polish.

"A *writer,* eh," he said. "That's a good game."

"Yes, that and volleyball."

"You ever write anything for *National Geographic?*"

"Well, I've been thinking of doing a musical about the
Gulf Stream, but right now I'm just trying to find the
best leisure village for my wife and myself."

"You've *come* to the best," he said. "I searched for ten
years before I decided to come here."

He was a retired insurance agent from Minnesota named
Dick Green, and he told me that he was sixty-two, six
years older than the average age at Sun City West. Although I knew that Sun City West was younger than Sun
City, I was still surprised to hear fifty-six; but there was
no doubt about Dick's figure: average ages were his meat,
as well as matching his jacket with his name.

"One member of each couple has to be at least fifty to come here," he said, "but it's really better if both of them are because contact with the young is . . . well, out of step with our style."

"But it doesn't *have* to be," I said. "Jesus said that children will own the kingdom of heaven. Will there be a *sub*kingdom for seniors there too?"

The devil was quoting scripture, but I was annoyed by his certainty that, after five thousand years together, the generations no longer mixed.

He laughed begrudgingly. "I'm not sure that children will be any quieter *there*. Look, don't get us wrong: we're *plenty* youthful here; you won't find any rockers around. We're what you call the *active* old. We feel younger and we live longer 'cause we're active all year round. If you don't get involved in something here, it's your own fault. And you know the biggest thing we're involved in?"

"Duplicate bridge?" I said.

"No, each *other*. We've got real community *pride*. We've even got a volunteer group called the Prides, who keep up the roads. This is the only place in the country where the streets are swept by guys who used to run companies. A former CEO cleaning out a drain, *that's* what I call America!"

"Jefferson should have lived to see it."

"And we've also got the Posse, our policemen. And the hospital has three hundred fifty patients and thirteen hundred *volunteers*. You think they've got that kind of public spirit in the places where they just play duplicate bridge? You know, some of the people here are still *working*. My neighbor works at the Valley National Bank."

"There are so *many* banks," I said. "Playing with your money seems to be the major sport here."

"No, golf is: eighteen courses and always packed. But the banks are fun too. Go into one tomorrow and you'll see what I mean. Try Western Savings; it's the best food."

"The best *food?*"

"Just go there; you'll see."

"So you feel that this place is definitely better than the ones in Florida."

"*Florida?* Florida's a *bummer.* You know the humidity there? And the *Cubans?* They're even worse. At least the humidity goes away in the winter." He let out a laugh at a line that must have brightened other church breakfasts.

"There are no Hispanics here?"

"They just wouldn't fit in. They're not Sun City people, if you know what I mean. A lot of these people buy their homes for cash, some for almost three hundred thousand."

"I'm sure some Hispanics could do that."

"They still wouldn't fit in. Oh, I know they like the heat, but you see, this place is full of top professionals, people who use their expertise to help the community."

"You're mostly Republicans, aren't you?"

"Of course," he said, as if I had asked if they were mostly alive.

"Then you know what you people *are?* You're Republican *socialists.* This place is an upscale *commune.*"

"I guess so, but this is a new world here, and it's what the guy said in *Future Shock:* You have to be able to manage change."

His words gave me a chill and I wanted to say, *Teach me how to manage change. How to look at old photographs without wanting to jump back into them.*

"Reverend," said Dick to a minister beside us now, "this is . . ."

"Ralph Schoenstein," I said.

"He's thinking of moving here."

"It would be an excellent move," the minister said. "This is the most caring place in the world."

"That's nice to hear," I told him. "Of course, they're caring just for their peers."

"Oh, no; some of the people have their own elderly parents living with them."

"But it's still entirely a community of white, middle-class seniors."

"Oh, we have our poor too, you bet." He sounded proud.

"Don't these people ever miss the *lower* generations? Some interaction with the young?"

"The young left us first, Mr. Shaughnessy. And we really don't miss 'em. Let me ask you: Where is the family today? Scattered. And who started the scattering? The *kids*. You know, there'll eventually be forty-five thousand people here — *mobile* people, remember that. But in the north, they just hole up in ice and snow. You see, this place is the logical result of the mobility that started after World War II. The soldiers came to Florida and Arizona and they saw that there's always sunshine here. They saw that the people are always upbeat and happy. Everyone keeps *smiling*."

Forty-five thousand relentlessly smiling faces, a drug dealer's dream, was a singularly sobering thought. Eager to see such mass contentment, I left the Lutherans, not for the Baptists but the bowlers in the nearby Sports Pavilion. And I almost didn't make it: while crossing the street to the pavilion, I was barely missed by a golf cart that came speeding around the corner. The obituary would have been offbeat:

> *Writer Killed by Smiling*
> *Christians after Prayer*

One of several big buildings in the R. F. Johnson Recreation Center, the Sports Pavilion had twenty-five billiard tables opposite twenty-five bowling lanes. I went over to one and started talking to a man of about seventy named Bill Fowler and his slightly younger wife, Peg, who had a puckish smile. It didn't seem quite the smile that the minister had boasted about, but he probably counted every kind.

Exiles from Canton, Ohio, the Fowlers had bought their $60,000 home here last year; and now they were semi–settled in, for they were one more example of leisure villagers out of sync.

"He likes the summers here," Peg told me, "but I hate 'em."

"Yes," I said, "I've met other couples who don't like these places equally well."

"That's true with most of 'em here," she said. "One loves it and one . . . well, so-so."

"Women are so *contrary,*" Bill said, having heard Peg after bowling his frame. "*You* love something, *they* don't."

"He thinks there's a big difference between men and women," she said.

"You a Libber?" he asked me.

"Well, I *am* for ERA. There's not as much difference as you think. Women are just irrational men — except *you,* of course, Peg."

She laughed and then said, "Listen, it wasn't irrational to be happier in Florida than here. But *he* hated it."

"I'm supposed to love bugs and mosquitoes?" Bill said.

"Well, *I* liked it there. We had more friends, and the place where we lived — Rainberry Bay — it was smaller and had more spirit."

"What'd I tell ya about women?" he said, poking me with his elbow.

"Of course, at *all* these places," she said, "you feel you're just waiting to die. They should've left some young people here."

"There were none here to *start* with," he said. "See what I mean about a woman's mind?"

"They're afraid of the young ones," she said. "A lot of these people hate children. They actually pulled *out* of the school district — the whole Sun City, I mean — so they wouldn't have to be taxed for the schools. Of course, not *everybody* feels that way. It really gets some of us down, an attitude like that. This one woman on our street got so depressed that she's moving to Phoenix."

"Probably just her time of the month — right, Bill?" I said.

"She's seventy," he said with a grin, "but women never really give that stuff up."

"Believe me, there's a *lot* of depression here you don't read about in the brochures," she said. "They're depressed 'cause they're bored with retirement and far from their kids. You should see all the drinking. And there are suicides too."

"Drinking and suicide are part of life," said Bill. "Peg, you're thinking too much, and that's not what a woman does best."

It struck me that a sensible move for Peg would have been not to Phoenix but to shoot Bill and take her chances at the singles' nights. However, she might not have done any better with another man because Bill was typical of his generation of American male, whose guiding philosopher was Fred Flintstone.

"It's a man's world here, isn't it?" I said to her.

"You bet it is," she replied. "The way the women go after the widowers! A single woman here just busts her ass to get a man."

"Peg!"

"He wants me to be a lady, like the other snobs in this place."

"Snobs?" I said. "In Shangri-la?"

"Shangri-*la*? *This*? Shangri-la sold to Chinese. *These* people, they're always lookin' down their noses at everyone. And don't ask me what these old army and navy people have to be snobby about." She rose and began moving toward the lane. "Excuse me, I'd better bowl or we'll be here all day. Which would be okay because there's nothin' else to do."

"She's really a good little girl," said Bill. "She volunteers at the hospital, you know."

"Where I was almost sent by a golf cart," I said.

"Oh, we had one *killed* by a cart last week."

"The place is one big asphalt fairway, isn't it?"

"Well, it's hard to practice your driving on the golf course 'cause it's all pretty straight."

"Like trying to practice your golf on the turnpike."

As Peg began to bowl, I looked at her with both sympathy and admiration. She was not going gentle into that good night: she was hollering in the afternoon. She was a feisty stranger in paradise.

A few minutes later, after saying good-bye to her, I was on my way to the snack bar when my path was suddenly blocked by a beefy man in a Western shirt, who had a sunburst buckle on his belt.

"Who are *you?*" he said, his stomach glinting at me.

"I'm just . . . looking around," I replied.

"Not any*more,* you ain't."

"Well, who are *you?*" He had met his conversational match.

"I'm a monitor and I want you to leave. We can't have people just looking around."

"But I might be *buying* here."

"You got any identification?"

"Sure — sure, *here.*" I whipped out my wallet and gave him a J. C. Penney card, which seemed like a mainstream credential to me, especially when it bore no indication that the October payment was overdue.

"Look, mister," he said, returning the card, "I still don't know who the hell you are and why you're wandering around, so you better just get your butt outa here."

Taking the hint, I left the pavilion and quickly walked away, past a car whose bumper sticker said

SUPPORT THE SHERIFF'S
POSSE OF SUN CITY WEST

Looking over my shoulder from time to time, wondering if Leisure Control had me under surveillance,

I walked a few hundred feet to the Sundome, a seven-thousand-seat center for the performing arts, where I slipped into a crowd that was waiting to hear Frank Yankovic, the polka king. I decided not to buy a ticket and to take my chances on the street. I would not let a pursuing posse drive me to hide inside the hall because I rated polka music somewhere between the sound of a tractor-trailer shifting gears and the sound of a cocker spaniel in heat.

On a bench near the entrance to the Sundome, I saw a tall woman sitting alone. There was something about the jaunty look on her thoroughly wrinkled face that drew me to sit beside her and introduce myself. She responded warmly, telling me that she was a Texan named Mary Nell Norton, who lived in Phoenix now, not here.

"I'm an odd duck 'cause most of 'em like it here, I think," she told me in a gravelly voice; "but I gotta be around young people. No, you don't have to ask me: I'm seventy-six, but I could go for *you* if you wasn't all bones. That's the style now, you know: older woman, younger man. 'Course, Ronald *Reagan*'s a younger man to me!" She exploded a laugh and then took a drag of her cigarillo.

"Before you take me," I said, "you should know that I'm a wanted man. The Sheriff's Posse doesn't have my support."

"Then come with me to the spa. That's where I have all my fun."

"The spa?"

"Yeah, in Phoenix; it's coed. And full of young people. They keep *me* young. I got cataracts but I still want action and this place is dead." She laughed lustily again. "*That's*

the truth! More deaths here than anyplace. From boredom, I'm sure. I could grab a man here if I joined the
casserole brigade."

"The casserole brigade? That's another paramilitary
unit?"

"No, whenever a wife dies, all the women bake casseroles and bring 'em to the widower with their names
and phone numbers."

I felt like an anthropologist who had found a remarkable tribal ritual. Had this ritual begun in 1960, when the
first leisure village was built here? Or had ancient woman
also sent mating signals with macaroni and cheese?

"They don't stay widowers very long," Mary said.

"But you're not interested in sending someone a little
meatloaf valentine?"

"Hell no, I'm happy just living with my dog and my
Higher Power."

Mary herself was a higher power. When it was time
for her to leave me and go into the Sundome, I felt so
good from having been with her that I walked slowly
across the square in defiance of that monitor; and suddenly I started to sing "O Who Owns New York?", a
song I had learned at Columbia College. I often sang
songs of my colleges, my summer camp, and my winter
army while walking down the street, a mental condition
on which a great deal of work was still to be done. I had
a problem described by John Cheever, who said that as
he grew older, he continued to think of himself as a
teenager, with the enthusiasms of youth. The maturation
process had passed over him, and over me too: at fifty-
one, I was still the boy to whom Mimi Kramer had softly
said in her living room one evening in 1949, "Ralph,

please get *off* me — my *parents.*" My father at thirty-five was more of an adult than I felt like now. What kind of a lunatic late bloomer was I? A blooming lunatic, that was all.

Driving out of the R. F. Johnson Recreation Center, I passed an old man in a uniform directing traffic, who seemed to be waving me away with extra zeal. Moments later, after passing the eight banks again and then a shopping center called Sundome Plaza, I left Sun City West until tomorrow and was back on the highway to the Kings Inn. To my left, set low against a cloudless sky, was a mountain range; and to my right was a range of billboards, one for Mesa's Leisure World and another with a grinning picture of actor Dick Van Patten:

DISCOVER WESTBROOK VILLAGE
ARIZONA'S NEWEST ADULT COMMUNITY

It seemed that the day was not far off when this land would be dominated not by the mountains but by the leisure villages changing colors in the sunset.

". . . so come to the Provinces," the car radio said, "the adult community that looks like New England."

America had become the land of opportunity in a remarkable new way. At last, people who wanted to move to Arizona but not have to *see* it could be shielded from the view by a floating Connecticut.

When I reached the Kings Inn, I took Lori to the pool, even more anxious now to squeeze every moment of delight from my days with a child who would soon disappear.

"Daddy, watch *this!*" she cried, but I was already watching too hard.

After the swim, we wandered indoors to a piano in the corner of a lounge, where Lori began to play "Yankee Doodle," one of the songs that she had been learning in her first piano course. To me, the sweetest sight in the world was a small girl seated at a piano, earnestly moving through a piece with carefully curved little fingers. Moreover, the piece Lori was playing should have been high on the Sun City hit parade, somewhere between "Happy Birthday" and "Amazing Grace." And, to crown the appeal, atop the piano sat Mindy, with her tiny legs dangling, like a stuffed chanteuse.

In spite of this concentration of charm in the corner of the lounge, one septuagenarian after another walked impassively by. I found myself angered by their lack of response, not just because of my pride in Lori but because I feared that the generations had become enemies now. I was looking for Norman Rockwell scenes in a Salvador Dali land, and I remembered what one of the bicycling women of seventy in Princeton had said to me: *The old connections are gone.* And I remembered the words of the principal of Hunter College High School, who had said, "This is the first generation of kids who have been cut off from the elderly because of age segregation."

At last, however, one woman came by and stopped at Lori and Mindy with an appreciative smile. To the accompaniment of "Yankee Doodle" and then "My Dog Fred," she told me that she was sixty-five, had come to Sun City from Wisconsin with her husband, and felt that it was heaven.

"It's such a protected little place," she said. "So warm and quiet and clean. And everything is done for you."

She had made it sound like intensive care with sand,

so I said, "But don't you think that the life here may be . . . well, a bit too bland?"

"Is it bland to live ten years longer?" she said. "That's what this place adds."

"But they're pretty quiet years."

"You want some other kind?"

"You have a point."

I thought of Helen Keller's "Life is either a daring adventure or nothing," but I decided not to argue with Lori's entire audience. Moreover, only a fool measured an ordinary person by the standards of an extraordinary one.

"You thinking of moving here?" she said.

"Maybe someday. I wonder how much of my hometown I'd miss."

"None; coming here is like being *reborn*. I mean, people come here to live out their lives and they wind up starting life all over again. I sure don't miss what it cost to live in Wisconsin. My husband and I couldn't have afforded to stay there with those taxes. No, you won't miss anything 'cause it's all *here*, especially the weather. I just *love* getting up in the morning and always seeing the sun. It makes my day."

"So you don't need a White Christmas. Tan is okay."

"I never want to see snow again. And to tell you the truth, I don't miss the crime either. It's so safe here that you can go away for two months with all your lawn furniture on the patio and it's still there when you come home."

"Yes, I guess in most places, the patio itself would be gone."

"Of course, we *do* have bandits here: the doctors. They

overcharge like crazy 'cause they think everybody's rich."
Turning to Lori, who now was playing a winged version
of "Salute to Octave C," she said, "Is this beautiful thing
your only child?"

"No," I said, "I have two other girls."

"That's nice; playmates for her."

"No, her playmate is me. The others are twenty and
twenty-four."

"I'll bet this one keeps you young."

"Everybody tells me that."

If the company of a child was the fountain of youth,
then why had the people here stopped drinking? When
the woman left, I pondered this thought; at seventy-seven,
William Steig, who wrote children's books, had said,
"You need a kid in your life somewhere"; and the thought
was still on my mind a few minutes later when Judy came
into the lounge. We gave Lori permission to browse in
the gift shop and then we sat down together on a couch.

"She's playing 'Salute to Octave C' like a teenager," I
said. "Do you realize that in only nine years, she'll be in
college and we'll be alone? Just you and I and Mindy.
We'll be able to start doing things all by ourselves."

"A life of our own?" Judy said with a wry little smile.
"That's pretty self-indulgent, I'd say."

"But be honest: *nothing* has been more fun for us than
the girls — right?"

"I wouldn't know. We've never *tried* anything else."

"Just nine years. God. The years are going so fast."
My eyes took on a mistiness that was either the look of
a poet or a basset hound. "You know the saddest line in
the language? 'This too shall pass.' "

"Except, of course, for a kidney stone."

I laughed. "I needed that."

"No, you need the Menninger Clinic." Her voice turned sharp. "Now listen, Mr. Nostalgia: if you plan to start reminiscing again, I'm going to get up and march right over there and start talking to that man about his bypass. It'll be fresher than another trip down memory lane with you."

"Okay, okay, I'll stay in the present." I turned toward the man who was my conversational replacement and I looked hard for some sign of life. "Jesus, that's too old to be. Let's really try to avoid that age."

"What you *won't* avoid is the funny farm. When are you going to stop all this ridiculous fear of getting older? Only *Mindy* stays the same age."

I smiled lamely. "Honey, believe me, *everybody*'s afraid of it. That's why plastic surgeons get to the Caribbean twice a year."

"Oh, not *everybody*."

"Didn't Sue tell you that the first thing she looks at every day is the obituaries to see the ages? And doing this book has made me even more aware of time. I mean, how did Willie Mays get to be fifty-three?"

"But don't you *see?* You're what's wrong with this country: your obsession with aging — with avoiding it, I mean, with always trying to stay young. That novel you wrote about finding a youth drug, the silly hero was really *you*. And all those *vitamins* you take. First E and then C and then brewer's yeast and then zinc. . . . What's next? Sheep-dip? Crazy Glue?"

She had me squirming now. I wondered if the exercise was good for my circulation.

"And pouncing on the *Enquirer* in the A&P," she said,

"to see if some woman of a hundred has had a baby, or if someone can remember seeing Lincoln."

"I take my hope where I can get it," I said, trying to lighten the moment but feeling ashamed.

"What you want to do is stop time. Well, life is not a basketball game."

"You must've heard that in Tibet."

"You know what I'll tell the divorce judge? That I've been married to Ponce de Leon. Who only found Fort Lauderdale, as I recall."

"But you've got to believe me, I don't *want* to keep thinking about all this: I'm just stuck with a terrible sense of time — and change and memory. Stravinsky said, 'A person lives by memory.' "

"You're a regular Bartlett's in justifying your craziness."

I decided not to tell her that Oscar Wilde had said America's tradition was its youth.

"Honey, what can I say? I'm stuck with this feeling — and I *hate* it — that everything's moving too fast. . . . The girls . . . the life we've had . . . the ruining of New York . . . my running speed. . . . It's all — I'm slowly losing *everything*."

"Me next," she said with half a smile. "And maybe not so slowly."

"I wouldn't blame you. I *am* acting just like Ponce de Leon."

"Then Poncey, open your eyes. Thousands of children are starving to death in Ethiopia. They're having their midlife crises at *three,* so I guess they won't be looking for wrinkles or clipping ads for Rumanian bee pollen. It seems to *me* that anyone who's allowed to get older should have no complaints."

"Yes, of course, of *course,*" I said, putting my hand in hers. "I felt stupid clipping that ad. And I *know* you can't trust the Rumanians any more than you can trust the Hungarians."

"Well, maybe their bees are okay."

"And maybe I'll be okay too."

"You better. The Menninger Clinic doesn't give financial aid."

We both were silent for a few seconds, and then she squeezed my hand.

"God, I'm a mental case," I said. "At least I haven't started singing 'The Days of Wine and Roses.' "

"Honey, *I* know how you feel," she said. "I heard 'English Country Garden' the other day and it made me so sad 'cause I remembered taking Jill to see Captain Kangaroo."

"That lovely song. She was two."

"And now they've taken him off the air."

"That's what I mean: nothing lasts, not the Morosco Theater or Mount Neboh Temple or even Captain Kangaroo. It's a disposable world."

"But you can't let it make you crazy. That look in your eyes whenever you hear, 'Where is the little girl I carried?' "

"Lori's almost too heavy for me now. My hauling days are ending; I've run out of thirty-pound girls. You know, sometimes I think I'd be happiest in a job where I could just carry little children around."

"Like kidnapping."

"No, I should've been a fireman. And it's also less risky than being a writer."

"You really *are* the catcher in the rye."

"Yes."

"But remember where he ended up."

For the rest of that day, while playing word games, shuffleboard, and poker with Judy and Lori, I tried to think of neither the future nor the past; just the sweet present here with these two, and an alternate present in Ethiopia. And late that night in the motel room, as Judy lay sleeping against me and Lori lay with Mindy in the other bed, I suddenly remembered the words of Jean Cocteau: "If you look back, you risk turning into a statue of tears."

The following morning, I drove back to Sun City West and stopped when I reached the strip of eight banks, the strip envisioned by the doctors when they made out their bills, the strip Dick Green had said contained a secret of Sun City's appeal. And so, taking his advice, I entered Western Savings and found myself in a lobby in the FDIC's newest chain, where the business of banking was elegantly camouflaged by sculpture, paintings, and trees.

At last, however, after passing an exhibition of Mexican watercolors and another of kachina dolls, I stumbled on something financial, a sign that said:

30-DAY MONEY MARKET CERTIFICATE	10.000%
91-DAY MILLIONAIRE ACCOUNT	10.900%
91-DAY MONEY MARKET CERTIFICATE	10.750%
6-MONTH ACCOUNT	11.000%

182-DAY MILLIONAIRE ACCOUNT	11.100%
1-YEAR MONEY MARKET CERTIFICATE	11.750%
3-YEAR MONEY MARKET CERTIFICATE	11.750%
FORESIGHT INVESTMENT ACCOUNT	9.500%
3-YEAR VARIABLE RATE CERTIFICATE	12.200%

As a man whose banking strategy was limited to simple overdrafts, I had never imagined that there were so many ways to make money at a bank. Not far from this statistical smorgasbord was another spread: in a carpeted lounge with a dozen small tables that was called the Westerner Club, a woman was offering breakfast and brochures for new accounts. On those mornings during my boyhood when sickness had kept me home in bed, I had listened to a program called "The Breakfast Club," on which people had been entertained by songs, riddles, and jokes; but here, forty years later, America's newest breakfast clubbers were finding sufficient entertainment in just spending the morning with their money.

About twenty-five people were having coffee and bullish dreams in this Westerner Club, which a person could join by maintaining a minimum savings balance of $12,500. Since my own savings balance was nicely stabilized at ninety-six dollars, and was in the name of Lori Schoenstein, these Westerners struck me as people in the upper middle class.

Near the entrance to the lounge, a man who was either an assistant manager or a maître d' told me that other banks in Sun City West had similar clubs, but the Westerner was the most popular.

"Because of its Danish or its certificates of deposit?" I said.

"Because we offer everything," he replied. "We're a social club where you can meet people and read the newspapers from back home. And members can also use the game room to play cards and free phones for local calls and free copying, safe-deposit boxes, and travelers' checks. We even have a jazzercise room."

It was like a USO, with coffee and doughnuts for the veterans of battles with American civilian life.

"Having a reason to stay in the bank all morning is good for these people," he said, "because a lot of them have time to kill."

What dismal irony, I thought. I was in panic because I feared that I was running out of time and these people were happy to be killing it. What human endeavor was drearier than the killing of time? For me, it was a capital crime.

"Is there enough money in Sun City to support all these banks?" I said.

"Two and a half billion dollars comes in to all of them," he said. "You see, most of these people had high incomes as professionals. Now they just keep bringing their money in and looking for the highest interest rates. They live off the interest."

"They live at the bank."

"Yes, we're a social institution now."

A few seconds later, he had to leave me to attend to bank business, probably a bridal shower, so I started wandering through the Westerner Club and eavesdropping on the killers of time. Pausing near two men of about seventy, I heard one of them say, "Bullshit! There's no such thing as competition. You have a goddam heart attack, you gonna start *shopping?*"

"It's the same with the undertakers," said the other man. "A guy croaks. You gonna start shopping?"

"A lot of people are going to cremation. It's cheaper. And nobody's gonna visit your grave anyway."

"I dunno. . . . I got a psychological block against being burned."

And I had a psychological block against this conversation. In spite of Judy's reminding me that I had not come from Krypton, I still had not filled out the organ-donor card with my driver's license, just in case a cure for death were found. If I ever did decide to be mortal in my early hundred and forties, after Lori had dumped me for her grandchildren, would I prefer cremation or burial? Surprise me, I decided, a thought from which I was happily distracted by a movement of breakfast clubbers out of the lounge and through the woods to a demonstration by a beautician from Roy's Hairstyling Salon of Phoenix.

I followed the people to the beautician and watched her expertise for a while; and then I turned to a woman beside me who happened to have blue hair and said, "This is the best hairstyling I've seen in the entire Federal Reserve System, but I'm pretty happy with the style I have now. I could, however, use some steam. Is there a sauna in the vault?"

"I don't think so," she said. "Just showers for the jazzercise."

"My name is Ralph Schoenstein."

"I'm Charlotte DuBoff, but you're too young for me."

"I'm married."

"Yeah, so many are. And you don't look like you're gonna drop soon."

"Have you lived here long?"

"I came from Chicago two years ago. I have the Montezuma."

For a moment, I thought she was referring to a troubled intestine, but then I realized that she meant the model of her home. The builders who named the models in leisure villages had a style as lyrical as the bards of Detroit, who gave us Eldorado and Malibu. This housing style, however, had been so influenced by England that both Concordia and Century Village had models called the Kingsley, an unfortunate duplication when Taj Mahal still had not been used.

"I'm getting a place in Rossmoor for the summer," Charlotte said.

"Because of the heat here?" I asked her.

"You could fry; it goes to a hundred and ten."

Since the summer in Florida also was not conducive to human life, such leisure village home splitting was becoming a common style.

"I'm curious about your routine here," I said. "I mean, do you spend all your time . . . well, just playing things or is there something special you do?"

"I don't *have* to do anything," she replied. "I've paid my dues."

"You used to have a job?"

She looked at me with a flash of irritation. "Don't worry, I've just paid them."

I had heard this testy reference to some phantom treasurer of the soul many times before from older people who had chosen to disconnect themselves from what John Donne called the main. In every leisure village, the new resident had to make a fundamental choice: either to blend his endless play and idleness with volunteer work or to be totally self-involved. Peg Fowler, my bowling friend, did volunteer work at the hospital here; but Charlotte spoke for most leisure villagers, who chose to be life's spectators in pampered seclusion.

"You're a widow?" I said to Charlotte.

"Yes," she said. "All I have out here is a sister at the Laguna Leisure World — in California. It's more expensive than this place, but that's because there's more security. And I have a cousin in the Leisure World at Silver Spring, Maryland."

The nuclear family was splitting into atoms that were settling in a growing network of leisure villages. I thought of the old song about "the dear hearts and gentle people who lived and loved in my hometown." To many people, "my hometown" was part of a franchise now.

"Do you ever find yourself missing children?" I asked her.

"Oh no," she said, "most of us don't. They can really take over a place."

"You mean the ones who come to visit on vacations?"

"Yes, everyone sighs with relief when they go home. Except this *one* woman down the street from me. You won't believe it, but she actually goes to the ice skating rink in Phoenix just to look at children skating."

"A real loony," I said.

When I had finished talking to Charlotte, I decided to leave the financial spa and take a look at the Montezuma; and so, I drove about a mile to the Model Home Center, a rotunda that contained an enormous model of Sun City

West. On a wall near the model was a painting of Del Webb, under which were the words:

Concrete, steel, and lumber make the buildings, but people make the community. Together we can realize a way of life unprecedented in America.

Gazing up at the painting, I felt as though I were touring Washington, for here was the father of the country.

"May I be of help to you?" said a salesman in a dark blue blazer, who had a boyish face but hair streaked with gray, the kind of bridge between the two worlds that I felt myself to be. "I'm Bill Beatty."

"I'm Ralph Schoenstein," I said with a pang of jealousy that I also couldn't have a name from a boy's adventure book.

"Are you thinking of buying here?"

"Yes, I want to get out of New Jersey."

"Doesn't everyone?"

"I hear nice things about the Montezuma."

"A lovely model indeed. Two independent bedrooms and bath suites, with a covered lanai, covered terrace, a kitchen with a breakfast room, and a double carport. Of course, it doesn't have an Arizona room, which you have in the Hopi."

"An Arizona room?"

"It's a second living room."

"And the Hopi's got it, eh. . . ." I paused for a moment of architectural reflection. Should I buy native Indian with an Arizona room or should I buy Aztec without one? "Of course, an Arizona room would really clash with a Mexican chief. I don't like Indian eclectic."

"The Montezuma does have an optional fireplace."

A fireplace in southern Arizona? Where the temperature rarely dipped below sixty? It had to be a hedge against a new Ice Age.

"Without the fireplace, what's the price?"

"Eighty-nine thousand, nine hundred now; but only eighty-five thousand, four hundred and five if you pay cash."

"Gee, if you only had caught me last *month*. . . . How long will the special be running?"

"Not very long, I'm afraid. Cash or not, all these prices will be going up at the end of the month — between eight and twelve thousand."

"That's quite a jump."

"Well, this *is* the world's premiere adult community, and the whole world seems to want to come here."

A few minutes later, I was walking through the models to which the whole world was beating a path. All were Southwestern-style homes with big sunny rooms, gleaming appointments, glass doors leading to patios, and names like the San Felipe, the San Angelo, the Nandina, the Kaibab, and the Moccasin; and on the living-room wall of each was a list of optionals similar to those I had seen at Clearbrook and Concordia. In the San Angelo, for example, a three-bedroom home, you had the option of irrigating your Arizona room with a wet bar; and you also had the option of closing your eyes to avoid seeing the big brown bearskin on the living-room wall, an ironic touch in a place where it was the people who were hibernating. Judy and I had always preferred less ostentatious animals on our walls, having enjoyed the ambience of squashed mosquitoes for many years.

As I walked into the San Angelo's den, past a standing

hourglass that was three feet high, I met a tall and bright-eyed man of not more than forty, who said, "Don't look at the decorations. They'll make you sick."

"Better here than somewhere that doesn't *have* total health care," I said. "You looking at this for your parents?"

"My mother. One of her friends came here and loves it. She rides around all day in her little golf cart. You know those things can go up to thirty miles an hour?"

"It's my favorite ride at Disney World. Of course, Disney World has no bank to play in."

"They sure do play in this place. But you know what I don't understand? This woman's been here for three years and she's already taken five *vacations*. How the hell can you take a vacation from a *vacation?*"

"It does seem to violate some law of physics."

"I told my mother she's probably better off staying in Scranton," he said. "There's snow but also people under sixty. But she says the people here like it, living with just their own kind."

"Gerontophilia," I said.

"What?"

"It's called gerontophilia."

"Sounds like something you should water."

"It's wanting to be with your own age group. Gray pride — and the hell with the young: we don't need 'em."

"You know, I just came from the Hopi reservation and they all live together in the same village — the young *and* the old — and they keep learning things from each other."

"The Indians don't understand the American way," I said. "I just came from a reservation in Florida called Century Village, where people in their *forties* are moving to get away from the young."

When this man and I parted after leaving the San Angelo together, I could not resist a return to the Sports Pavilion for another talk with Peg Fowler. The pavilion's parking lot today had many more cars than yesterday, mostly Cadillacs, Caprices, Buicks, and Lincoln-Mercurys. Inside, however, there was an even bigger change: every one of the twenty-five bowling alleys was in use. For a moment, the time was out of joint for me: I could not accept this scene on a Monday; but then I remembered that every day was Sunday, with only hymns to identify the official one. At the Sports Pavilion, and everywhere else in Sun City West, and everywhere else in the twenty-three hundred retirement communities of America, it was Sunday, Monday and always.

I could not find Peg, so I just stood at the wall, beside a sign that said NO CHILDREN UNDER 6. Watching all these Monday bowlers bowl, I thought of Pleasure Island in *Pinocchio,* and I felt as Lori had on the final day of the second grade before the start of summer vacation, when she had written, "School is over. I feel sadish-happyish." Much of this journey through the world of the American dropout was leaving me sadish-happyish too.

"It's *you* again!"

The voice of the monitor shattered my thoughts.

"I was looking at a *model!*" I quickly said. "*Really.* Call Bill Beatty in sales. *He'll* tell you how I fell in love with the San Angelo. I'm just taking it with caribou instead of bear."

His eyes were still suspicious. "I dunno. . . . You don't look old enough to be here."

"You've made my day," I said with a smile. I could skip my brewer's yeast today.

But suddenly I knew that my pleasure in his perception of my relative youth was just another sign of the disease that had put me perilously close to insanity: the disease that drew my eye to the age of every man I read about before I read anything else, that made me jealous if he was younger than I was and happy if he was older.

You pathetic jackass! I thought. *You colossal jerk! You American!*

I belonged in an asylum. I would go to California.

The Forecast:
Golden Rain

PART IV

The call came into the medical clinic of Leisure World at Laguna Hills at 10:25 one night: a woman was choking in her apartment. Nurse Susan Boyd took the address and moments later arrived to find that the woman was all right but the bed where she reclined was all wrong: it belonged to a man in his midseventies, who had already taken care of her windpipe and pleasanter parts as well.

"Half of them are living together but aren't married," Susan Boyd told me as I sat in her office at Laguna Hills, where 25,000 people lived in a place built by Ross Cortese, who had built the Rossmoors and several other Leisure Worlds too. Unlike Del Webb and H. Irwin Levy, Cortese was an unseen rearranger of the old. There was no Cortese Boulevard here and he appeared in no commercials to be shown to people buttering bagels. There was just his first name as part of the Rossmoors, and not even that in the Leisure Worlds he had built in California, Arizona, and Florida.

"A lot of these people do get married, of course," Susan said, "but they live together first, just like the young. One woman called and asked me if I'd do premarital blood work for her and the man. I asked for the addresses, expecting two different ones, but she said, 'Do I *have* to tell you I'm living in sin?' "

"It's nice that someone still thinks of sin," I said, "in a country where renting pornography is now a homey way of life."

"The art for these people is hypochondria. They hate to hear that nothing's wrong with them."

"I've seen it; they like to enjoy ill health."

"And they use it to get service too. One man actually faked a heart attack just to get a plumber for his drain. A lot of these people overreact, especially the ones who don't do much, the ones with all the time on their hands. Some of the others do volunteer work and they're in better shape. They don't panic."

"Yes, it's sad to see them panic," I said.

The hypocrite had spoken again: the man who was in panic *creatively* because he saw himself drifting farther and farther from his family photographs. If I ever came to Leisure World, I would need my *own* nurse: to make sure that my stomach didn't rise into my chest from an overdose of brewer's yeast, to stop me from singing "When You Wish upon a Star" in buses and banks, and to put me back to sleep at three in the morning when I woke up reeling from the terrible randomness of things and wondering why the holidays felt hollower every year.

"The problem is," said Susan, "that when they call with an emergency, you can't really believe what they say on the phone. The other day, a woman called and said, 'My husband is dead on the toilet.' But when I got there, he wasn't.''

"Dead or on the toilet?"

"Neither."

"Well, it's hard to be dead on a toilet. You need a great sense of balance."

"Which these people don't have."

"They fall a lot?"

"They do. And throw themselves out of the golf carts too."

"I saw golf-cart daredevils in Arizona."

"A few weeks ago, one poor man almost killed himself. He hit a tree."

When I left Susan's office after our talk, I saw that trees were hard to hit at Laguna Hills because they were hard to find. Ross Cortese had put a sprawling urban overlay on this piece of Southern California: dozens of apartment buildings starkly stood beside streets unrelieved by greenery. And in the center of all this charm was a high dark building that was a Western salute to Stonehenge. Who, I wondered, would come to Southern California to live in a tower? It was like going to Bora Bora to bowl.

I wanted to visit the sales office now, but I had lost my bearings, so I stopped a tall thin woman of about sixty-five and asked for directions.

"Just follow me," she said in a bright New England voice, and then she told me her name was Martha Corwin.

"How's the life here?" I said as we walked.

"It's not unpleasant. They wouldn't allow it to be.

Still . . . every time I leave, I feel like a bird let out of a cage. Of course, I'm an old Yankee crank who doesn't really belong here."

"Do most of the others like the cage?"

"Oh, yes; they don't have to work to keep it spruced. And they love all the planned activities. Everything's so *scheduled*. Do you know that book *Escape From Freedom?*"

"Yes, I've read it," I said, pretending I had. For thirty years, I had meant to read it but been lured to other scholarship, like *The Illustrated History of the National League*.

"Well, I think a lot of these people were secretly unhappy with the freedom of the world, especially when they got older. What's scary out there isn't just crime."

"Were you an English teacher?"

"Art — and I still am. I teach part-time at Laguna Beach High School. I taught in Brookline and then my husband died and my children talked me into coming here. But escaping from freedom was a mistake for me."

"What's that big tower over there?"

"The Tower. That's what it's called."

"Sounds medieval."

"It's for people who need constant medical care. You see, it's really four stages, I'm afraid. From the outside world to Leisure World, and then to the Tower, and then to a lower accommodation."

"Speaking of that last one, I think I'm staying in California so I won't have to see that cheerful little ad *The Times* keeps running on the front page: FOR THOSE FAVORING CREMATION."

"*Favoring* cremation?" she said.

"Sounds like a straw poll, doesn't it?"

"Are you afraid of dying?"

"No more than anyone else. I'm terrified. But I'm working on it."

"Well, stay away from here; dying's a major activity, and the only unscheduled one. They call this place God's Waiting Room."

"I've heard that in Florida too. But this is the first place I've seen with facilities for people who get too infirm to live in their houses."

"Yes, that's good, I guess. But it does make you so aware of the whole business of breaking down. I suppose the thing to do is just ignore death and try to grow old gracefully."

"I *hate* that phrase," I said with an anger that surprised me. "Why is *grace* so important in aging? For Baryshnikov maybe, but not for me. If I can swing from trees, I will!" And, of course, I had the mentality that would have been comfortable swinging from trees.

"Gracefully or not, it's foolish to do your growing old in America. You know what Hemingway said: 'There are no second acts in American lives.' "

"That was Fitzgerald."

She laughed. "You see why I teach art. Anyway, this is a second act and the country doesn't like it. You know, *I* drink Pepsi and even wear jeans, but you never see *me* in those commercials. And I'm certainly skinny enough. Lord, so are *you*."

The American goal was to be young and thin. At least Martha and I were halfway there.

When we reached the sales office, I said good-bye to her and entered what was called the Golden Rain Administration Building, which sounded like the weather bureau in Shangri-la. I decided to stop at the desk of a woman named Joan Hickey, who had short blond hair and purple lips.

"My name is Ralph Schoenstein," I told her, sitting down. "I'm thinking of moving here."

"The wisest people are," she said with a smile.

"I've already been to New Jersey, Florida, and Arizona. I'd like to know why California is better."

"Well, New Jersey, of course, doesn't count; and Arizona and Florida are unbearable in the summer. In fact, people are moving *back* from Florida."

"How is this place better than the Leisure World at Camarillo?"

"That's a Leisure *Village,* not a Leisure *World,* and there's no comparison."

Leisure Village. Leisure World. What was next? Would older Indonesians soon be heading for Leisure Archipelago?

"Why is there no comparison?" I said.

"Because Leisure World has *much* more recreation. It's the whole Cortese concept."

"You mean fun with security? Secure fun?"

"Yes, there's an ideal balance here. Also the weather. A friend of mine managed Leisure Village and he says it's just too hot up there."

"What's the minimum age here?"

"It used to be fifty-two for both partners, but the governor just signed a new bill: one partner can be *any* age. There's quite an uproar about it. In fact, some of the women in our Seal Beach community even want to picket the statehouse."

"They must be in shape."

"Our exercise programs are the best in the country."

"What's the religious blend here? I'm Jewish."

"Oh, Jews are quite comfortable; they're about thirty percent. One of my dearest friends is Jewish."

"One of mine too," I said, thinking of Judy, and also thinking that in fifty-one years, this was the first time I had ever heard this line spoken nonsatirically; but then I remembered that this was California, where surrealism was the norm.

"What are the financing arrangements?" I asked her.

"For a cooperative, you pay cash," she said. "Between forty-five and ninety-five thousand, and a membership fee of sixteen hundred for our recreation fund. The monthly payments are about three hundred, depending on the type of manor you pick, and this includes principal and interest, taxes, insurance, cable TV, water, trash, and all outside building and grounds maintenance."

"Sounds good," I said, having not the slightest notion what all those things were worth. I was trying to affect an air that would keep her from knowing that I was constitutionally unable to learn the difference between a cooperative and a condominium.

"But I have to tell you," she said, "that the monthly payments are about to go up."

"I always seem to arrive on the last day of the sale."

"Yes, don't we all?"

"Well, at least you get a nice new home."

"No, there are no new ones: it's all resales now. But don't forget the marvelous tax break you get when you sell your old house: a tax-free profit of a hundred twenty-five thousand dollars." She pointed to a page on her desk. "Say, *this* might be something for you: a condominium for one thirty-four in a three-story building with underground parking. The Catalina. Two bedrooms — the master is twelve by fifteen — two baths, a balcony, a carpeting allowance, and a fireplace."

It was the same fireplace I hadn't wanted in Arizona. Who built *fires* in Southern California, where it was seventy on Christmas Day? A fire would clash with the central air conditioning and leave you with — what? Perhaps the feeling that you were coming down with malaria.

"For a condominium," she said, "you pay either all cash or with a loan after a minimum down payment."

Neither method of payment was appropriate for me because my budget happened to be structured for a state lottery win. Nevertheless, I wanted to take a look at the place, so I left the office with Joan and walked to her car in the seductive California air.

It was a day to be bottled. Birds were singing on the barbed wire of the walls and a golden sun was shining on six pools, seven clubhouses, ten sentry points, and meetings of the Cribbage Club, the Rod and Gun Club, the Duplicate Bridge Club, the Retired Dentists Club, the Astrology Class, the Calligraphy Class, the Organ Class, the Nifty Fifties Club, the Swingin' Sixties Club, and the Stroke Club. I wondered if the members of the Stroke Club were showing slides of their CAT scans.

"This was nothing but orange groves and bare fields in 1964," Joan said.

"You've nicely upgraded all that," I said. "By the way, I presume no children are allowed."

"Not to live here, no; but one *was* smuggled in. We

found a woman with a son who was going to the University of California at Irvine."

"A pretty nervy enrollment."

"Of course, he wasn't really the kind of child our people object to. It's the younger, noisier ones. Still . . . ."

"I'd like to talk to that woman after I leave you."

"Security won't give you a pass for that. You have to stay with me."

"I'm afraid I've already wandered a bit; I talked to the nurse."

"You should've had a security clearance. If you buy a home here, you won't want strange people wandering around, I'm sure."

"Yes, sorry about that. You know, in spite of my break-in, I heard at Sun City that the security here is terrific."

"Absolutely," she said, unlocking her car. "Some of the gates close at eleven P.M. and you can't get through them again till seven in the morning. And the apartments even have special screens to keep outsiders from looking in."

Suddenly, I was assaulted by the roar of a jet fighter that would have skimmed the treetops had there been trees.

"Now *that's* security," I said.

"They're from El Toro — the base," she said, quickly adding, "but our people don't seem to mind."

As I was entering her car, another jet fighter shattered the air. On both the highest and lowest levels, from protection against Russian attacks to the prevention of peeks into kitchens, this bit of the California coast was secure.

Or was it? I began thinking now about those women at Seal Beach, the Leisure World a few miles north, who no longer felt secure, who were in rebellion against the State of California; and as Joan drove me toward apartments called Casa Rosa, Casa Contenta, and Villa Reposa, I was picturing not sunny patios and blood-pressure screens in breakfast nooks but these rebels. Their outrage was not the first turmoil I had found in leisure land: the first had been the attempted expulsion of a woman who had sneakily given birth; but this turmoil seemed more momentous than one triggered by surreptitious reproduction, for the new California law allowing one partner to be any age was a crack in the very foundation of leisure land as a safe retreat from the young. It was one thing for a woman of forty to have a baby here. It was quite another for a man of sixty to move his baby in.

The following morning at ten, I left the house where Judy, Lori, and I had been staying and drove down the coast to the Leisure World at Seal Beach, which lay behind a giant globe, as if the entire earth would soon be a summer camp behind a sentry booth. And perhaps it would, for the Japanese were copying New Jersey's Concordia, and anything the Japanese made was likely to become a standard for Man.

"I'm going to the sales office," I told the guard at the gate.

"The sales office?" he said. "You look too young."

It was another shot of rejuvenation for me, one that I realized I could repeat whenever I was feeling older than was allowable in America. I could simply drive up to the leisure village sentry and take a sweet slug from this fountain of youth.

Beneath the familiar barbed-wire walls, I entered the compound, a smaller and older one than Laguna Hills, and parked outside another Golden Rain Administration Building. And then, in what had become an accomplished move for the Wandering Jew, I casually strolled past the office and on to the golf course, just in time to see a man climb out of a water trap.

"Henry, I *told* you to take the stroke!" cried the partner of the soggy sportsman. "You almost fell in that one last *week*."

"So I don't have to use the pool today," said Henry with a sheepish grin; and then he saw me approaching. "Mister, you got a towel?"

He was a short man with tufts of white hair at the sides of a shiny scalp, and he wore a shirt whose alligator had never been more appropriate than now. I introduced myself, told him my mission, and he replied, "This place is the *greatest!* There's never a dull moment!"

"Where did you come from?" I asked him.

"The water."

"No, I mean your original home."

"Long Island. Port Washington."

"You ever miss it?"

"I miss my home, sure — but then I remember how much work it was. The smartest thing I ever did was get rid of that big house. The people are friendly here, I play golf every day, and I even make love to my wife."

"You fall down doing that too?" said his partner with a grin.

"There should be *more* of this living for the elderly,"

Henry said. "It's got medical attention, games, *everything* to pacify us. If we're on the outside with younger people, we interfere. The world is for the young."

I had barely heard his thoughts about the young because the word pacify had derailed me. I was startled to hear someone say that an entire generation of adults should be handled like hyperactive children.

"Are you as happy as Henry?" I asked the partner.

"Well, *I* am," he said.

"And who isn't?"

"My wife. To tell the truth, she could kill us all."

"Why?"

" 'Why?' he asks me. How do you ever know why a woman's unhappy? She misses her friends, I guess, and her big house."

"Sometimes it takes a while to get used to this place," Henry said. "The couple next door to me, they came from Minnesota. With them, the *husband* didn't like it. But he got used to it. You can get used to anything."

"Speaking of unhappy women," I said, "I hear there's a bunch of 'em here who're pretty upset about the new age law."

"Sure, who wants rock music?" the partner said.

"It's more than that," said Henry. "They don't want to see the men bringing in young tootsies. So now they want the governor's balls — not that they'd know what to *do* with 'em anymore." He began to laugh.

"You're a sex maniac, Henry, you know that?" the partner said.

"Yeah, but I'm better at golf. At sex I need a bigger handicap."

"G'wan, you're in shape," the partner said.

"Well, at least I don't go running to the doctor just to *talk* to him."

"Yes, some of 'em do that," the partner told me. "Some of 'em, with nothing to do, they just like to complain. It's mostly the widows, they're lonely. They need Henry."

"They're a little crazy," Henry said. "You know what I saw one of 'em wearing the other night? A fur coat, an evening dress, and *support* hose! Who takes *that* to bed? A psychiatrist."

"I'll head for the clubhouse now," I said. "It was nice talking to both of you."

"Just remember we don't even lock the doors here," Henry said. "I wouldn't live outside unless I wanted to be mugged. Even with the crazy ladies, this is the place!"

When I left this damp Don Juan and his friend, I walked for about a hundred yards along the edge of the golf course, past a long line of bungalows that looked like those I had lived in at summer camps. Over their doorways were signs announcing such all-American couples as JIM AND DOTTIE BROWN, DON AND ALICE YORK, and CAPP AND CONNIE CONSTABLE.

Now don't start singing camp songs, I told myself. Look to the *future*, not the past. But could I be happy in the future that awaited me here?

Stopping at one bungalow, where a man in a forty-niners cap was reading *Forbes* on a tiny porch, I tried to imagine life in an endless summer at Camp Cortese, behind a sign that said RALPH AND JUDY SCHOENSTEIN. . . .

"*Good morning, darling.*"

"*Morning.*"

"*Another day without cold, kids, or crime.*"

"*Yes, I'm afraid so. Is there anything new?*"

"You bet. The Cholesterol Club is taking a field trip to picket a dairy."

"Darn. It conflicts with a meeting of the Parcheesi Club and I'm running for office."

"I didn't even know you were in it."

"It's the last one I'm joining. The Camera Club, the Table Tennis Club, the Genealogy Club, the Gadabouts, the Spanish Club, and the Feeling Good Club are all I can handle. I need some time to enjoy *myself too."*

"So you've decided not to join the Jolly Mixers?"

"The Gadabouts have more dimension. We mix, but we're not always happy about it."

"Say, I've *got an idea: let's go to the doctor for a checkup."*

"No, let's save that for Saturday night."

"You know what I'd really *love?"*

"No, what?"

"To see a pine tree."

"Oh, so would I. Maybe the Evergreen Club has some slides."

A few minutes later, in one of the rooms of the clubhouse not far from a main room full of bridge players, I sat at a table around which a dozen white-haired women were busy sewing and stewing. I had stirred them up by mentioning the governor of California.

"I certainly won't vote for that stupid man again!" said a woman with plump cheeks and rimless glasses, who could have adorned a candy box. "I'd understand if he was a *Democrat* 'cause they always do awful things, but he's a *Republican* doin' this to us! I mean, it just isn't *fair* to have teenagers here. That's why we move *in:* to get *away* from 'em."

"I just don't know why he'd *do* such a thing," said another, who was sewing a dress to be sent to a retarded child, perhaps in her teens. "It'll be the *end* of these places, I tell you. We might as well live outside, even though you can't *live* outside."

Sitting at that table, amid all those white heads that could have been a Norman Rockwell painting called Stitch and Bitch, I realized that their fear of the young had led them now to a civil war; but in this one, there was no combat: they only retreated from the enemy.

"But . . . are you ladies afraid of teenagers as somebody's *children* or . . . as somebody's *wives?*" I said, politely tossing the hand grenade.

"*You* know old men!" one of them said. "They'll marry 'em *any* age!"

Soggy Henry had been right: the new age law was a threat to every decent woman on the wrong side of menopause, a blow to age segregation as strong as the Supreme Court's blow to segregated schools. The women at this table could not bear the thought that widowers would now ignore their casseroles to salivate over less aged meat.

"It makes me want to get out of this state," said another bit of old lace. "Maybe I'll go with my sister. She's in Florida, at that Red Buttons place."

"But Florida could pass the law too," I said, and she looked at me in silent dismay.

Hearing these women condemn the young while making clothes for them, I felt a rush of pity and I found myself saying, "Would you like me to help you write a letter to the governor?"

"Oh, *would* you?" one of them said.

And as I took out a pencil and pad, a roomful of collaborators began to work with me:

"Tell him this is our way of *life*."

"Tell him the young people don't want to be with us *either*."

"Tell him we can't stand *noise*."

"Tell him how much we've *paid*."

I felt like Thomas Jefferson, for these women wanted nothing less than independence from the generations below. Instead of the words I was putting down, I should have been writing:

"When in the course of human events, it becomes necessary for one people to dissolve the bonds which have connected them with another . . ."

The problem seemed to be that in America today, the bonds most precious were those paying nine and three-quarters percent.

Early the following afternoon, I left Judy and my playmate and I began driving north through the San Fernando Valley toward Leisure Village at Camarillo. I was anxious to see if the attitudes were different at Camarillo, which I had heard was the finest leisure village in California. This commercial had come from someone who lived there, a man of eighty named Arnold Lehman. I had learned in a phone call that he was highly intelligent, a former professor of history at Columbia; and so, I was on my way to a place called Pleasant Valley to see how one historian's mind had adapted to this American revolution.

My own mind was still having trouble adapting to a

car radio, for during the drive, I found myself once again being tossed between memory and desire.

"When I was seventeen," Sinatra was singing, "it was a very good year . . ."

Helplessly, I surrendered to the old bittersweet ache — but then suddenly pulled myself back and said, *Stop* thinking those years were better than these! When you were seventeen, you were terrified of polio and Jimmy Berman died in Korea and it still took you three minutes to unhook a brassiere. When you were seventeen, you had the tentative lust of one nervous girl: you didn't have the love of Judy, Lori, Eve-Lynn, and Jill.

A turn of the dial now brought me, "Only last July, when the world was young," and I turned again before my longing could build. The women at Seal Beach were afraid of the young and I was afraid of memories of them.

One more turn brought me, "Lavender blue, dilly dilly," and I remembered Lori's imitation of an old lady this morning. I had laughed, but her mimicry had made me uneasy too, even though becoming an old lady wasn't one of my worries. I would be a senile teenager first.

What the hell generation was I *in* anyway? Wasn't it time to officially join one? Perhaps the answer was not to be frozen like the Seal Beachers but to stay socially freewheeling. My friend Mike was thirty-six and my friend Fletcher was seventy-two and *both* were my contemporaries; but were such friendships coming to an end? America was a battlefield now, with people like Helen Hayes and Ashley Montagu fighting for intergenerational living against H. Irwin Levy and Ross Cortese, who were merrily packaging seniors.

Near the end of the Ventura Freeway, I passed a billboard with a picture of a policeman, who had one hand up to slow me down:

A SAFE RETIREMENT IS AHEAD
LEISURE VILLAGE
SANTA ROSA ROAD
CAMARILLO

At 6:30 on an October morning, Arnold Lehman awoke in the three-room condominium for which he had paid $50,000 six years ago, for which he now paid $109 a month for maintenance, and which resembled 2,150 other condominiums in Camarillo's Leisure Village, where there were 504 single women, 37 other single men, and one writer doubled up on a couch that was too short for him. I had spent the night on this couch in Arnold's living room, between his stereo and his leatherbound set of Dickens, because I wanted to follow him through a day in what was becoming the new Our Town.

A few minutes later, at the Formica table in Arnold's small kitchen, we sat facing each other over orange juice, while I kept sweeping his cat out of my lap.

"Stay *off* him, Homer!" Arnold said. "I'm afraid he likes you."

"Oh, that's okay, he's cute," I said, pretending that I enjoyed the pouncing of paws on my genitals. This circulating cat had been making me angry until I realized that he was Arnold's roommate, his only constant companion in this gleaming leisure world. On mornings when no nosy writer awoke with him, Arnold drank what Larry Hart had called orange juice for one. Could *I* ever live alone like this? I was chilled by the thought. Life's good moments did not even *exist* for me unless I shared them with Judy or one of my daughters: they were like trees falling in an earless forest. If unthinkable luck ever delivered me alone to a house like this, I would need more than a cat for company: I would need Gunther Gebel-Williams.

"I'm just about the oldest man in this place, you know," Arnold said, "but I don't *feel* eighty — whatever eighty is supposed to feel like."

I was not about to reply, *You're only as old as you feel* to a former professor from my college, so I lamely spoke the alternate cliché: "You don't look eighty to me."

And he didn't: he looked eighty-five. His face was a crosshatching of lines, his neck was widely spotted, and his hair vestigial; and yet his eyes were bright and his mind seemed as sharp as it must have been thirty-five years ago when we were both at Columbia. "It is terrible to find one's intellectual passions mocked by the passage of time," Ronald Blythe had said in *The View in Winter,* and I wanted to add no unintentional mockery of my own, especially toward someone who had been on the same faculty as my mortal god, Mark Van Doren.

I did find Arnold's clothes, the Izod shirt and madras pants so popular in leisure land, to be slightly jarring, for the retired professor as preppie was disturbing casting to me. However, didn't a man of eighty have the right to look the way he wanted? Many of the leisure villagers, especially those in their billowy Bermudas, looked like parodies of the L. L. Bean catalog; but I had never believed that clothes made the man, especially when I had seen photographs of Mahatma Gandhi.

"It's better that I'm in this place, you know," Arnold said as we finished breakfast. "At my age, I'd be a problem to somebody sooner or later."

"I am right *now*," I said, wondering if being a problem was not still a part of life rather than a reason for escaping it. Ronald Blythe had said, "Any adjective that can be applied to a person in the prime of life can be applied to a person of seventy, eighty, or ninety: contrary, sexual, noble, spiritual, weary, exalted, messy, muddled, happy, accepting, denying, grouchy, and pleasant." However, seven years ago, Arnold Lehman had left the world in which his two sons and five grandchildren lived and had come to this place where his very imprisonment gave him new freedom to take a midnight stroll.

"What do you do all day?" I said, suddenly thinking of Martha Corwin.

"I read, listen to music, tape my biography . . . and swim and play tennis and bridge," he said. "And I chase women, especially the ones not chasing me. No, don't look startled. Sex for us doesn't descend into farce any more often than it does for the young. Sometimes the earth even moves — when there's a quake, that is. My students had to laugh at stuff like that; you don't." He stood up. "If you're finished, we'll join the parade of walkers. That's how I start every day."

"People are out this early?"

"Oh yes, by seven. Usually I hear Bach on my Walkman, but today I'll listen to you."

"The thing is, Arnold, I've just got to project and see if this life would be right for my wife and me. She takes no walks at seven A.M., I'll tell you that."

"When she finally gets up, what does she do?"

"She's a teacher."

"Teachers can stay active. Some of them hold classes right here."

"She does remedial reading."

"That would be one of the smaller classes, I'm afraid."

When we walked out of Arnold's house just after seven, the rising sun was pouring such intoxicating light on the condominiums that I felt God was in His heaven and all was right with Leisure World.

"What a beautiful day!" I said.

"It's always a beautiful day in California," he replied. "This climate is like the Riviera."

"A day like this makes me forget the Shakespeare sonnets about decay and think of Mark Van Doren and his optimism."

"A great man, Van Doren."

His saying this made me realize one of the advantages of living only with people your own age: they know all your references and never think that Pearl Harbor is a new rock star.

"Van Doren knew that the world was full of terror," I said, "but he felt it was still too wonderful not to love. He had us ignoring the terrors and looking at the beauties."

"And that's the thing about this place," Arnold said. "We've screened out the terrors and kept the beauties." He glanced at a woman approaching us. "Of course, this isn't one of them. . . . *Hi,* Edna, how are you?"

"Good morning, Arnie!" said a woman of about seventy with a small pink bow in her two-toned hair, pink pedal pushers, a blouse that looked like the cover of a seed catalog, and lipstick that came close to following the outline of her lips.

"This is Ralph Schoenstein. He's thinking of coming here."

"Come on *in!*" she said, sounding like a commercial for a pool. "You'll live longer — and so *relaxed*. There's no sweat about anything — except when I try to get this man to lectures with me."

"I *gave* lectures for forty years," said Arnold with a patient smile.

"Not like *tonight's,* you didn't: 'Sex and the Senior Citizen.' "

"Is he for or against it?"

"I don't know; let's find out. It's a *she,* a gal named Carla Rusk."

"Sorry, Edna, I have duplicate bridge."

"Wanna compromise and go to the dance?"

"Sorry, duplicate bridge."

"Oh, *poo,*" she said, moving on.

"I'm afraid she wants to play duplicate bodies with me," Arnold said as we continued to walk. "But I feel sorry for her, she has no car. The ones with no cars can't get to the village unless someone takes them — for restaurants and shopping and things."

"How far is the village?" I said.

"Four miles away. I often walk it at this time, but we'll just go to the clubhouse today."

"You know, fifty doesn't mean what it used to, and I see that neither does eighty."

As we walked, Arnold greeted other walkers and bicyclists too. There was something about the sight of a person on a bicycle, especially a person of seventy, that made me feel good; it was a sight full of breezy hope.

Now don't patronize them and say you like old cyclists, I heard Helen Hayes saying. *Some of these people are just as rotten as the average teenager. They're just* people, *nothing else.*

However, some of these plain people had reached the new American life span of seventy-four. How many of them saw themselves pedaling on borrowed time? How many had freed themselves from the thoughts of age that haunted me?

When Arnold and I entered the clubhouse, a man in a shirt whose V plunged sharply across a hairy chest came quickly toward us. He wore a tiny transmitter on his wrist.

"Arnold, you *heard?*" he said.

"Heard what?" Arnold replied.

"The women in V Twenty-two: they were *arrested:* they're *hookers!*"

"V Twenty-two . . . V Twenty-two," Arnold said, trying to envision this site of the ultimate leisure.

"The one with all the little blond curls — and the daughter living with her, the one with bad skin."

"Ah, yes. Friendly people."

"To half the valley."

"So the skin wasn't that bad after all. How'd they get caught?"

"The guard at the gate saw so many men coming in he got suspicious."

Arnold smiled wryly at this revelation of the one rec-

reation that the planners had overlooked. "Well . . . there
are so few good positions for a mother-daughter team
outside of show business."

"They were doing it for *months!* Imagine! We never
knew."

And then Arnold started to sing, " 'Both mother and
daughter, working for the Yankee dollar.' "

It was a fragment of "Rum and Coca-Cola," a song I
had stumbled through at a high school dance in 1946, and
I was aware again how pleasant it was to be with someone
who had all your references. Intergenerational life *did* produce comments like, "Is it true that Paul McCartney played
with a group before Wings?" and "I didn't know that
Omaha had a beach."

"And just think," Arnold said to me a few minutes
later as he walked through the clubhouse, greeting friends,
"Edna wanted me to go to something as academic as a
lecture about it."

"What was that thing on his wrist?" I said. "That
button."

"For medical emergencies. It's worn by people who
might need sudden help. It reaches the hospital, which
then tells the main gate and the paramedics come. They
can make it in a couple of minutes."

"What happens to the people here if they get too sick
or feeble to stay?"

"They go back to their families. In Florida, a lot of
them move back even when they're not sick; but they
don't leave *here* that way."

Arnold now talked for a while to one of the directors
of The Leisure Village Association, who said the new
annual budget was four million dollars. Many members

of this association, owners of Buicks, Bentleys, and Cadillacs, had sold their old homes for three or four hundred thousand dollars and then, for two hundred thousand, had bought homes here that required no overhead. Moreover, because of California law, these new homes were taxed not at their current value but at their quaint purchase price.

After hearing enough of this talk to feel that I had taken a vow of poverty, I went back with Arnold to his overheadless, undertaxed house, where he made two calls to women living alone. The first call was in his capacity as a member of Neighbors Care, for the woman was one of several who required a daily check. And the second one was a mating call. He talked to the woman for a couple of minutes, finally saying, "Good, I'll come over and see you splashing around." Then he hung up and told me, "She's someone I see — a widow." He smiled self-consciously. "Man is not made of wood."

"Of course," I said, profoundly encouraged to see a man of eighty whose loins had not become a petrified forest.

A few minutes later, after feeding his cat, Arnold turned on his television set to the Leisure Village cable channel for a program that taught bridge. Sitting beside him, I watched players showing how to bid and play hands; and once again, I was aware that I might not fit into an adult community: I was fifty-one and my favorite card game was still crazy eights, which the cable channels seemed to ignore.

When the bridge lesson was over, Arnold and I both read books for almost an hour, and then we went to the clubhouse pool for the exercise class of his female friend.

While a tape deck played Mozart, an instructor in her twenties with a blond ponytail led ten women through calisthenics in water up to their waists. The women, who seemed to be in their sixties, bent and stretched and twisted with zeal, turning *The Marriage of Figaro* overture into an aquacade. I wondered why they had to work out in water, for they weren't swimming; but then I realized that exercise was the new religion in America and reason was not applicable to holy ritual.

One of the exercisers, whose plump face was crowned by a bathing cap covered with rubber petals, waved to Arnold.

"That's Dottie," he told me. "My younger woman."

"May I ask how much younger?" I said.

"Sixty-three."

"She's really peppy."

"Don't sound surprised. We're not different, just slower."

"May children use this pool?"

"No, not the pool or the golf course."

"Same as Century Village."

"If you think this is the same as Century Village, you have a serious problem in perception. That's a low-class operation there."

When the class was over, Dottie dried off and sat with us beside the pool.

"I've got cellulite on the run," she told me. "And I hate you for not having any. Such skinniness should be illegal."

"I'm afraid I can't help it," I said. "It's my metabolism. I had it checked once and I burn up more than I take in."

"Then you should have disappeared by now," Arnold said.

With a laugh, Dottie squeezed his thigh and said, "Isn't he *cute?*"

"She has a profound respect for both my mind and my thigh," he said. "That's because neither has cellulite." Dottie laughed again and he smiled lovingly at her. "A happy spirit, this lady."

"Why not?" she said. "I mean, this is the happiest time of our *lives.*"

"You really feel that, don't you?" I said.

"Of *course.* The children are on their own, we have no money worries, and we have more activities here than we can handle: games and lectures and classes, you *name* it." She turned to Arnold. "Oh, by the way, the Nakonas are leaving."

"I'm not surprised," he said. "This is no place for Indians. They miss what they had."

"*American* Indians?" I said with surprise.

"Yes, one couple."

"This does seem like an odd place for them; they like to keep the generations together. I saw that in Arizona."

"Well, they *don't* like living with a tribe of old Republicans who need lectures on 'Sex and the Senior Citizen.' "

"I take it we're not going," Dottie said.

"Let's just do the homework," he said, patting her hand.

At noon, after a long session of sunshine and laughter with Dottie at the pool, Arnold and I returned to his house, where we ate tuna fish sandwiches to a Brandenburg Concerto. Then he went into the bedroom to take his daily nap, while I sat in the living room with a book of poetry, still seeking the answer to the proper way to grow old. Soon Longfellow was telling me:

> For age is opportunity no less
> Than youth itself, though in another dress.
> And as the evening twilight fades away,
> The sky is filled with stars, invisible by day.

And then, sustaining the celestial theme, Palladas said:

> Try and grow used to the place of every star
> And forget your own dark house.

But how many people in leisure villages were looking at the stars? So many of them — and not just the hypochondriacs — seemed to be looking inward, not outward. However, didn't they have a *right* to look at their X rays instead of the stars? I could hear Judy saying, *Stop telling these people how to live. At least* their *checks* clear. Moreover, Arnold had shown me that it was possible to live an active physical and intellectual life in a leisure village. Suddenly, I thought of the unpoetic words of Dr. William Menninger: "The way to achieve mental health is to find a mission in life and take it seriously." But after having seen eight different leisure villages, I still couldn't say if any of them would provide a mission to sanity for me.

A few minutes after two, Arnold and I walked to the platform tennis courts for his daily doubles game.

"They all cheat," he said. "Foot faults. But no one calls it. We're happy our blood still reaches our feet."

As we approached the courts, we met a stocky man

about six feet tall, whose white tennis shorts revealed bony legs.

"Hey Arnie," he said, "I got one for ya. Did you know I had sex almost every night?" He paused for a moment with a gleam in his eye. "I almost had it on Monday, I almost had it on Tuesday, I almost had it on Wednesday. . . ."

"Terrible," Arnold said, overrating the joke a bit.

The comedian was a man named David Berg, a lawyer of sixty-seven who once had been a tennis champion in Ohio. When I heard this background, I felt a sudden craving for exercise that could not be satisfied by a still-life sport like platform doubles. Moments later, he accepted my offer to play tennis singles. However, while he was getting a racket for me, a cloud passed over my delight, for I realized that I was about to play someone who was sixteen years older than I.

Once again, I was oppressed by thoughts of age: there was no escape for me, even on a tennis court. In spite of Berg's Ohio title, he was now nearing seventy; my beating him would be expected, my losing to him would be a disgrace, and his coronary would be a nice test of the emergency medical service here. I wondered if he had stayed in condition by ever playing mixed doubles with the mother and daughter in V 22.

As our match began, I felt a paralysis of will. Should I try to beat this remnant of a champion by running him? Should I honor the grand American tradition of trying to break his back? Or should I respect his age and carry him by playing a mediocre game, which came easily to me?

The hell *with his age!* I thought. For years I had been told that age was only a state of mind; and so, I decided to play him as a comrade under the clock, and I won the first two games with placements that I rationalized as aids to his circulation. In the third game, however, he warmed up and beat me, making me happy for him. When he beat me again in game four, I was less happy for him; and when I lost game five, in spite of one reckless charge that sent me lunging into the net, I rose sportsmanlike to the challenge with the thought, *Okay, you ambulance chaser, get ready for the ambulance to chase* you!

As our furious battle continued, I tried to enjoy the thought that I might be able to play like Berg in sixteen years. However, I couldn't play like him *now:* he had the strokes of a former champion, while all I had were the legs of a man who ran against his daughter. With all of my lunatic pride on the line, the match turned into a clash between his arms and my legs: he was driving, slicing, and dropping balls all over the court, while I was running to retrieve them with the style of a man being chased by a Doberman. Our rallies were some of the longest in which I had ever made wind sprints.

It was five games for his arms and five for my legs when he stopped in the middle of one point and put his hand to his head. Faster than ever, I ran to his side of the court, going around rather than jumping over the net because the score was still tied. My previous thoughts about his condition, mere idle amusement before the match, suddenly seemed to be grimly true. When I reached him, his face was red and he was sucking air.

"I'm afraid I'm overdoing it with you," he said between quick breaths.

"Of course; we'll stop here," I said, graciously not mentioning that he had defaulted. "Are you okay?"

"Oh, I'll be fine."

"I'm sorry about all the running; I'm so used to racing my little girl. I never seem to be with my own age."

"There was a time. . . ." he said wistfully, and he needed to say no more.

Leading him off the court to a bench, I remembered one leisure villager telling me that he wanted no children around because he wanted to be with his peers. And peers were the people I should have allowed Dick Berg to continue to beat. Our match had hardly been a triumph for the intergenerational life.

Fortunately, his face quickly changed to the proper color, his pulse dropped below two hundred, and soon we were sitting with Cokes in the clubhouse. When I happened to tell him about my search for a leisure village and the disturbing feelings about children I had found, he said, "You hear about that new case in Florida?"

"I've heard about a couple of Florida evictions," I said.

"No, this one is special: at a place called The Woodlands; it was on TV last week. They're evicting a couple that had a baby, but — and get this — they're allowing *another* couple to keep a pet *monkey*. And the monkey's twenty *pounds* — bigger than the *baby*."

"Jesus, no kidding; that's incredible. They'd rather have a zoo than a nursery?"

"That's what it says in the deeds."

"But you think these deeds are Constitutional?"

"I dunno. You can't restrict for race or religion, so the question is: Do children have the same rights as blacks and Jews?"

For the rest of the day, during this drink with Berg, during the time at Arnold's apartment when he put more of his autobiography on tape, and during the dinner with him in a Camarillo delicatessen, I thought about the baby and the monkey. And I wondered: Were American *children* an endangered species now? What kind of society produces people who want their toddlers to be apes?

At nine o'clock that night, after a friend at *The Miami Herald* had given me the name of the family being evicted from The Woodlands, I made a second Florida call.

"First of all," said Bonnie Pomerantz, mother of the illicit ten-month-old Erika, "we had no idea that the restriction was in the deed and a *lawyer* checked it for us. But the really outrageous thing is that grandparents are raising other children right here and they're throwing *us* out. These are vicious people, I tell you; they *lied* in court. They said that only our section — section one — was paying court costs, so the judge said the children in the other sections couldn't be discussed. The truth is *every* home in Woodlands is being assessed to get us out. And we have a whole *yard,* so noise from Erika couldn't *possibly* bother them."

Moments later, her husband Ron was saying, "There are *three* monkeys, not one, and there's a two-year-old with her grandparents down the street. It's selective enforcement and it makes no *sense:* these people should be so *happy.* I mean, they're really rich and all they do is eat and play cards and play golf."

But food and cards and golf did not seem to be enough. A loaf of bread, a deck of cards, and eighteen holes in the wilderness had produced a disturbing pettiness in people who should have been mellow. Once again, I asked myself: Could Judy and I be happy there? Presuming I found a way to import cocaine and buy one of the homes, and presuming we learned to play bridge and golf, would we want to be with people who preferred Bonzo to baby? Arnold Lehman's life at Camarillo's Leisure Village was the most attractive one I had seen; but this sudden view of a dark side of leisure villagers had made me want to look for another way to spend what Browning called the best of life.

"You need a reason to get up in the morning," my grandfather used to say. Perhaps the reason should be something more than making sure that the world is exactly the same as it was yesterday.

Every Day Is Matinee

PART V

"**D**o you ever wish you could be a little boy and grow up again?" Lori had asked me on the flight home; and I had wanted to say that most of the little boy still was there, one who played crazy eights instead of bridge, touch football instead of golf, and bedroom garbage instead of living room chess. Now, a week after leaving California, I was back in the neighborhood where I had officially been a little boy: the streets off Broadway between the Ansonia Hotel and Loew's 83rd. I was on my way to see Molly Stahl, a widow of seventy-seven, whose leisure village was called Manhattan.

"Would you like to be younger?" Lori also had asked, proving that age obsession can be inherited, and I had replied almost sincerely, "No, I'm happy to be what I am; *every* age is good." Today on these noisy New York streets, I was looking in opposite directions on the path of age: both back to my boyhood and also ahead to the time of Molly Stahl. As I turned west from Broadway into 76th Street toward Molly's old apartment house, a parked car pulled out and I remembered a stickball game when tagging third base had suddenly become a challenge to me because the base had driven away. I remembered a silver-haired man in a checkered jacket who liked to be our umpire; and, once in a while, he even had played, giving one of the teams its own bookie. The intergenerational quality of these stickball games was further enriched by the elderly doormen, who put down their beer cans long enough to retrieve foul balls; by the nursemaids, who graciously refrained from pushing babies into double plays; and by the grandmothers, who paused at the baselines to offer such sporting strategy as, "Try not to get run over, boys."

Molly lived on the sixth floor of a building from which high drives by pull hitters sometimes caromed into Broadway, sending the center fielder across the trolley tracks and into another game. When she led me into her one-bedroom apartment, where programs for concerts, plays, and films were scattered on tables in the small living room, I found myself with a short woman who moved quickly and whose gaze was warm but intense. Although her hearing was good, her face leaned towards me and her eyes widened whenever I spoke, the kind of interest I had hoped for whenever Judy stifled a yawn.

In Molly's living room this morning was a man of sixty-eight named Morty Goode, who was wearing a backpack and hiking boots.

"Do you plan to scale the Ansonia?" I asked him as I sat on a couch beside fliers that said WHAT THE NAVY ISN'T TELLING THE PEOPLE OF NEW YORK and KEEP NUCLEAR MISSILES OUT OF OUR BACK YARD!

"Morty bikes all over," Molly said. "He picks up tickets for us and he also takes food to old people."

"Like us," Morty said with a smile.

"If *he's* old," she said, "I'm Mount Rushmore."

"You two see a lot of plays?" I said.

"All we can," she said. "Plays and concerts and movies — sometimes two or three a day."

"How do you afford it?"

"We see mostly the free ones. Morty and I have very little money, but so many wonderful things are free, or nearly. Last week, we saw a new opera for two-fifty, and that same day we had a free concert at the Lincoln Center Library."

"*And* the Equity Library showcase of *The Bells Are Ringing,*" Morty said. "After which this woman reads all night."

"What stamina!" I said. "Don't you get tired?"

"Yes, waiting on those long lines in Times Square for the cheap tickets," she said. "And sometimes I do fall asleep in the theater; but then Morty nudges me and I wake up and I swear I understand the play better than some people who were awake all the time."

"Perfect equipment for a critic," I said. "You know, you two belong in the *Guinness Book of World Records:* 'Most Entertainment Absorbed Since Nero.' "

"We do get around," she said. "You see, we belong to a lot of places, like the Museum of Modern Art, so we know all the goodies available every day."

"Nice to meet you, Ralph," said Morty, getting up. "I have to be going now."

"You having lunch with me at JASA?" Molly said.

"No, I'll meet you at the museum for the Kurosawa."

"You want to see that Strindberg thing at the Public Theater tonight?"

"We'd have to get in line at six and the Kurosawa might not be over."

"All right, see you at the museum. Don't get run over, dear."

So they're still saying that, I thought.

After Morty had left, Molly made tea for us and then said, "We're part of a subculture, Morty and I; but what a lovely subculture it is. I wish you could have seen all the free theater in Central Park last summer — and there's so much *street* theater too."

"Too much of New York is street theater," I said. "Theater of the absurd. It's why so many people leave for the leisure villages of Florida and the West."

"Then they miss the fifty-cent lunches at JASA," she said, and we both laughed. "They miss a life of being — well, Morty and I, we're really free souls. We even belong to a thing called Audience Extras. You call up and a tape tells you what shows have cheap preview tickets. Sometimes you'll pay three dollars for a forty-dollar seat, but that's all we can do. Morty lives on his army disability pension. Luckily his rent is frozen."

"So is *he* on that bike, I'll bet."

"No, we don't mind the cold. I guess that's why we're not really old. That bike and my feet are right for our budget. You see, all *I* have is Social Security and a little savings. We're a pretty modern couple, don't you think? Older woman, younger man. My children don't approve, but my grandchildren do, and my great-grandchildren will too when they learn to talk, which you see hasn't been a problem for *me*. You know, my mother lived to a hundred and three; I'll have to show you the poem I wrote when she hit a hundred. But first, how'd you like some *wonderful* cider I just got at a farm? I'll get you some." And she jumped up, her body heading one way and her mind darting in multiple directions like a water spider. "Look at the photos in that Adams book I just picked up. *Incredible*."

A few minutes later, with Molly wearing a light overcoat in a temperature of forty-five, we left her building for a noon lunch at the West Side Senior Citizens Center of the Jewish Association for Services for the Aged, a name H. Irwin Levy would have changed to Song of Solomon City. As we walked east towards Columbus Avenue, through streets where I had pursued balls and girls, Molly told me that both she and Morty were JASA volunteers.

"He'd be helping to set up the tables today," she said, "but he has to take lunch to a woman in his building, the Lincoln Towers. Terrific building — right next to Juilliard. You want to come to the Symphony Theater tonight? It's wall-to-wall Bach."

"I might; Bach's my favorite," I said. "You know, I was once thrown out of the Symphony Theater: by an usher when I was ten."

"How exciting. Why?"

"My guess is it was for throwing Goobers at girls in the children's section. I have better relations with women now — I think."

"The children's section. Yes, I remember those. Now the children are making the movies."

"And the country has sections for the adults. Molly, have you always lived on Seventy-sixth?"

"No, I had a big apartment on Riverside Drive and Eightieth, where my two children grew up. Then my husband died ten years ago, but I just couldn't leave the neighborhood. It's so vital and so *exhilarating*."

"You aren't afraid in these streets?"

"Well, I don't always walk; I use subway and bus. I was only mugged once, by two young guys who snatched my bag. I chased them to Riverside Park, but they were too fast for me. But I'm glad they went that way because I love Riverside Park. I go to see a community garden there every week."

"What a spirit you have!" I said to a woman who would have called the Black Hole of Calcutta a pleasant place to get out of the sun.

When we reached the JASA building on 68th Street off Central Park West, Molly went to a table in the lobby and bought two one-dollar tickets for a concert at Carnegie Hall; and then we took some stairs to a basement social hall, where lunch was being served.

In this big room, whose bare walls and long brown tables would not have set Red Buttons singing, people in their sixties, seventies, and eighties were carrying trays of food to their seats. After paying a dollar for two meals, I waited on line for them with Molly and then we went to a table, where she was welcomed by four other women.

"I've decided Morty's too old for me," she told them. "Meet Ralph Schoenstein."

"Where's the rest of him?" one of them said. "Don't he ever eat?"

"*You've* been eating his share, as we all can see," said another.

Molly introduced the women to me and I tried to remember their names, but I was distracted by the aroma of the food, which took me back to Fort Dix; and when I bit into a piece of brown meat, the taste lived up to the promise of the aroma. Seeing my effort to swallow meat that may have been partly mineral, Molly said, "This brisket hasn't been cooked enough."

"For fifty cents, you expect cracked crab?" said a woman whose name may have been Sally. "You see, Ralph, with food like this, we have to be tough to survive."

Sally then told me that she had become a sculptor upon retiring from teaching and recently had given a one-woman show.

"Here's my brochure," she said, giving me one. "The stuff's for sale, if you happen to like second-rate sculpture."

"G'wan, she's *good,*" Molly said. "And such *energy.*"

"Don't think that all old people are old," said the woman beside her, who then told me she had just learned folk dancing and had gone to a nursing home to entertain.

"Tell him how your son is trying to turn you on," Molly said.

The woman smiled. "My son, the pothead, he said, 'Mom, why don't you take a joint once in a while? It'll lift you up.' So I tried one. I'm still at the same elevation."

"Me *too,*" I said. "I tried it once; no effect. I get more lift from Excedrin."

"Oh, Excedrin's nice. It's a good trip."

"And if you want to kick it, you can switch to Anacin,

which has less caffeine. You know, there should be a
halfway house that can bring you all the way down to
Bufferin.''

"Would one of you junkies please pass the ketchup?''
Molly said. "Ketchup is what this brisket needs.''

"The potatoes could use some too,'' I said.

And so, here I was with a new sculptor, a new folk
dancer, and a relentless aesthete, all of whom were in
their seventies and all of whom were too high for drugs.
As I sat over food that was ready to become pop art, I
learned that many of the people here today lived in single
rooms in hotels, but all found adult education, travel, and
volunteer work at JASA, a place dedicated to keeping
them off the streets of Florida. And I learned that some
of these people, like me, had friends in all eight decades.
In fact, after telling me about her trips to read to sick
children, one woman said, "I love all the programs here,
but there *is* one thing I miss. I miss ever hearing someone
say, 'Did you hear? So-and-so just had a baby.' ''

The very words spoken of Bonnie Pomerantz.

During coffee, one of the JASA officials came by and
I told him about my tour of leisure villages.

"They're gorgeous, those Edens,'' he said, "but recreation isn't enough; these people need community in-
volvement, and they need younger people too. Those
places are very busy and beautiful. Also very lonely and
empty.''

"But don't they live longer down there?'' I said.

"Just the opposite: it's been proven that people who
disengage from society *shorten* their lives.''

"Speaking of shortening your life, is lunch often like
this?''

He smiled. "Survival of the fittest, wouldn't you say?"

As Molly and I left the room and walked upstairs, I thought of Sun City's Peg Fowler and Mary Nell Norton. They would have liked it here — if, of course, they could have sent out for lunch.

When we reached the lobby, a man called out, "Hey Molly, you were great last night!"

"Thanks, Sid," she called back.

"That's a pretty personal remark for a lobby," I said. "Does Morty know about him?"

"He's talking about the play we did here last night: *The Sunshine Boys*. And he's being polite: I was lousy; but so was everyone else."

"Real ensemble playing," I said.

It was the Seventh Avenue subway, that rolling pistol range, that took Molly and me to Local 237 of the International Brotherhood of Teamsters on West 14th Street for her two-o'clock class in creative writing.

"I know you're tough," I told her as I scanned the car for people on parole, "but a *teamster*."

"Not a truck driver," she said. "I worked for the city and this place is for retired municipal workers. There's classes, trips, shows — everything to stretch your mind. Sometimes I write for the newspaper. Last week I wrote about my TESL kids."

"Your TESL kids?"

"At the International School; I'm a volunteer. I teach English to a couple of kids from Taiwan."

"Molly, you're too noble for me."

"Well, you have to give something back."

"With most people, it's bottles. You never considered moving to Florida?"

She replied by reaching into her handbag and pulling out a small piece of paper. "Here, read this. I did it for our class poetry magazine."

Whenever I enter a crowded bus
A young woman offers her seat.
I accept, secretly pleased.
Validation of my justification
for remaining in New York.

My Florida siblings and children
Query as the years go by,
"What are you waiting for?"
I reply, "I love New York.
In Florida, people ride in cars,
With no chance to smile
At the chance encounter."

"That's good," I said. "I like the double use of 'chance' at the end. You weren't afraid to use it twice."

"I couldn't think of anything else."

"The only problem is, of course, that the chance encounter in New York can be with a thirty-eight. There are teenagers on these trains who aren't going to violin lessons."

"Oh, I'm a teenager *too*," she said, and again she opened her handbag, where I saw a book called *Ninety-Five Free Things to Do in New York*. This time the paper she produced was imitation parchment:

LOCAL 237 TEAMSTERS

Retiree Activity Committee Diploma
Molly Stahl

*This certifies that your spiritual
outlook has resulted in adding to
your longevity and you are now a*

RECYCLED TEENAGER

*Fun loving, charitable, patient, neighborly,
involved, sociable, and a seeker of knowledge.*

"That certainly tops what I got from Columbia," I said, and then I thought: *Isn't turning a seventy-seven-year-old woman into a recycled teenager too patronizingly cute?*

Here it was again, the native American disease: the highest praise for Molly was to make her a teenager. Had there ever been a time, in ancient China perhaps, when teenagers had been praised by making them honorary elderly? And what irony there was in flattering an adult by dubbing her one of America's current teenagers, those semiliterate lovers of rock videos and video machines, who seemed bent on proving that evolution could be reversed.

A couple of minutes after leaving the subway at 14th Street, Molly and I reached the headquarters of Local 237 and went upstairs to a small classroom, where she embraced her teacher: a man in his early thirties with tousled hair, elbow patches, and an unlit pipe in his mouth. He seemed a man more likely to be stirring up estrogen in the Ivy League than to be teaching at Teamster Tech. Seated with him around a table now were Molly and eight other students, all more than sixty years old.

"Welcome, people," he said. "We'll be talking about Jonathan Swift today and I'm going to have you write ironic editorials; but first, read any good poetry this week?"

"Yes!" cried Molly. "Shakespeare's sonnets."

Damn: she had to remind me of those unbearably beautiful flights about the passage of time that I kept trying to forget. Why couldn't she have spent the week with *Casey at the Bat?*

"There's nothing better," the teacher said. " 'Bare ruined choirs where late the sweet birds sang.' "

"I don't like Sylvia Plath," said a man in a windbreaker.

"Why not?"

"Too morbid."

"Yes, she's not a lot of laughs."

"You think she's famous 'cause she killed herself?"

"Well, suicide never hurts a writer's reputation. But I think that Sylvia Plath would've gotten there by hanging around."

I was wondering about suicide as a way to promote my next book when I saw it: on a chair by the wall, a newspaper lay open to a full page ad as unforgettable as those bare ruined choirs:

BABY BOOMERS
You're Not Too Young
for
Heritage Hills
of
Westchester

While the class began a discussion of Jonathan Swift, my mind turned toward Westchester. There was one more leisure village I had to see. And I feared seeing it as much as I feared remembering those sonnets.

Junior Senior

PART VI

The name sounded like a memorial park: Heritage Hills; but when I drove into this gateless community set in the woods of northern Westchester, I saw two children of about ten playing platform tennis.

Are they visiting grandparents? I thought. Or are they living with parents? Or are they about to be taken to court?

Driving toward the sales office, I saw that Heritage Hills, unlike Laguna Hills and Concordia, was part of the countryside and not a replacement for it. And, unlike Clearbrook, no photographs of the outdoors were needed: tall trees and shrubs were everywhere; and, in the distance, legitimate hills could be seen.

Inside the sales office, I found brochures for one- and two-story condominiums called The Stratford, The Canaan, The Armonk, The Guilford, and The Katonah at prices from $115,000 to $250,000, with monthly maintenance fees that went as high as eight hundred dollars. These hills were alive with the sound of money.

From a table in the reception room, I picked up a *Weekly Activities Bulletin* and learned that the Happy Hoofers were about to resume their sessions, that the Ukrainian Easter Egg Workshop would be meeting next Tuesday in Club Room 2, that the Appliqué and Quilting Workshop was now being taught by Beverly Shapiro, that the Woodcraft Workshop could be joined by calling Tom Daly in Condo 3, John Little in Condo 8, or Bob Weissman in Condo 12, and that Indians of the Southwest would be discussed in the Game Room on Monday afternoon. The rest of the curriculum had a little less of the liberal arts than the Teamsters.

After a while, I drifted to the desk of a woman in sales named Rose Siegel and I introduced myself. Responding as if I could have afforded to live here, she said, "Schoenstein. A nice German name like mine. Yours means pretty rock."

"Yes," I said, "I'm a Rhineland Rocky."

"And what can I do for you?"

"Well, I've been looking at leisure villages in Florida, Arizona, and California, and I'm wondering why this one is better than all of those."

"First of all, it's a different *concept*. This isn't a retirement community — there's no medical facility here — and more than half our people commute to work. Our average age is fifty-five, but going down fast." She lowered her voice. "You're Jewish, aren't you?"

"Of course. Like you, I presume."

"I look like an Arab? What I'm saying is: those Jews

in Florida, they don't *do* anything. The goyim out West, at least they volunteer. But the people *here* don't have to volunteer because they're still part of the *world*. Half the time they're in New York, and it's fifty miles away."

"Some of those leisure villages are building shopping centers right on the grounds."

"And so are *we* — but we're still preserving the environment. Just try to find the environment at those places. Tell me, are you an empty-nester?"

Another of the new pigeonholes. In America, the seven ages of man had become: preschooler, Pepsi generation, baby boomer, midlifer, empty-nester, senior citizen, and organ donor.

"I have one out of the nest, one half out, and one still being hatched," I said. My avian metaphor needed work, but I never thought clearly when the subject was departure from my nest.

"Well, whenever you come, there'll be a place for you. We have fourteen hundred units right now, and another sixteen hundred units are being built."

I had never grown used to "unit" as a description of a home. My unit had been K Company of the 60th Infantry Regiment; and I could not imagine Sinatra singing a hymn called "The Unit I Live In." Nonetheless, if I were going to survive in the new America, where a convent in the Bronx was being turned into a condominium, I would have to accept the fact that everything I saw, no matter how leafy or lovely or grand, was simply a condominium in progress.

"Your ad about baby boomers," I said. "I don't understand it."

"What's not to understand?" she said. "We're inviting baby boomers to come and live here. Believe me, a lot of them can afford it."

"But they're in their mid*thirties,* maybe tops thirty-nine. Isn't the minimum age here higher than that?"

"Oh no; it *was* forty, but then the state legislature outlawed *any* age requirement — it becomes discrimination — so the minimum age for all the new units is eighteen."

Eighteen. *Eighteen. Eighteen?*

We talked for another few minutes, but I barely heard her words. I think she said that this corporation had communities in Connecticut called Heritage Sound, Heritage Cove, Heritage Glen, and Heritage Fen. It was hard to hear anything she was saying over the sound of my mind screaming *Eighteen.*

"Of course, there still can be no children," I think she said.

When I left her, I went outside, almost bumping into a woman who was jogging with impressive speed, and I began to walk down the road to the clubhouse. But now I wanted to think, not see; I was trying to absorb what I had just heard. I should have been good at absorbing absurdity by now. It had taken me just a few hours to accept the fact that the wife of the head of the Soviet Union had gone shopping in London with an American Express Card; and the Heritage Village requirement that owners had to be at least eighteen was on the same surrealistic level as Madame Gorbachev's charge account.

For many months, I had been searching for the best leisure village by visiting places that secluded the oldest

Americans; and now the journey had come to its end in a place full of the elderly of all ages. It was true, of course, that Heritage Village was half composed of people who worked, but nevertheless I had to ask: Why would people in their twenties or thirties retreat to *any* cloistered society? If they had the money to buy a house here, then they were in the flush of both youth and cash and the entire world was open to them. They could be making Ukrainian Easter eggs in the *Ukraine*.

I was pondering this baffling business when two men who seemed in their twenties came from the opposite direction and I heard one of them say, "I'm going down to Mount Kisco today. Who knows what tomorrow will bring?"

Yes, I thought, seize Mount Kisco today, and Yonkers too, for the uncertainty of tomorrow has grown terrifyingly big.

It is hard enough to make order out of chaos when the chaos is static, Hunter Thompson had said. *It is a superhuman task when the chaos is multiplying.*

Therefore, perhaps you could not blame young adults for becoming early-blooming seniors, for backing away from the chaos to a condo colony. Perhaps these young adults were less alive than people their age used to be, but a rage to live was now less important than a sensible life-style.

When I reached the clubhouse, I went inside and smiled nervously at a guard in a little room to the right of the door.

"I'm buying!" I said like a barroom sport, and he waved me on. I was about to take a look at the usual arts-and-crafts rooms when I was startled by the sound of a basketball, an alien sound in an adult community clubhouse, and it drew me down the hall to a little gym that contained half of a basketball court. On this court, moving sharply and shooting baskets with style, was a ruddy, white-haired man of about sixty and a boy of about sixteen. Was this a grandson visiting his grandfather? Father and son roommates? Or a prospective buyer considering early retirement as one of his post–high school options?

"Wanna play some one-on-one?" said the man. "Start with him and I'll play the winner."

"Sure," I said, glad that I always wore sneakers. "Just let me shoot a few to get the range. It's been a while since I've gone to the hoop."

As the white-haired man threw me the ball with an easy snap of his wrists, I wondered which of these two I could beat. And I decided neither: the man was too smart and the boy was too fast. Also, the boy was too smart and the man was too fast.

Trying to impress them, I began to toss up shots, all of which were out of my control.

"Just looking for the range," I said; but in forty years of looking, I still hadn't found it.

Switching to lay-ups, I drove for the basket as if I were racing with Lori, and I almost made the shot.

"Fellas," I said, "I don't know if I'm up to one-on-one today. I played a lot of tennis last week. How about some horse?"

They agreed and we began the game of matching baskets called horse. The man was older than I, the boy was younger, and I felt a little like both. As we started to play, I thought of the ladies of the Seal Beach sewing circle, one of whom would have been telling me, *Just play with the man. Let the boy go out and steal cars.* I had, however, become convinced that the blend on this basketball court was precious and had to be saved from the leisure-village revolution, which encouraged the old to fear the young, which cheated the old of the spirit that life with the young produced.

"She'll either keep you young or kill you," a friend had told me when Lori was born in my forty-third year. I seemed to have stumbled into the happier course of the two.

In touring the leisure villages, I had seen many good people caught in the revolution, some gladly going with it and some swept along reluctantly; and faces and voices came back to me now as I tossed up air balls in this little gym. . . .

Mary Nell Norton of Phoenix, who merrily marched to her own drummer and not in the casserole brigade, and

Martha Corwin, the mellow Yankee crank, the displaced person, the blithe prisoner of Laguna Hills, and

Dave Berg, my Leisure Village tennis foe, who almost had a posthumous score, and

Ella Klein, my queen of King's Point, who had managed to hold her dignity while dancing with me, and

Jan with the tattooed number, my entire concert audience at Century Village, who had a heart of steel and an ear of tin, and

Peg Fowler, the spunky Sun City bowler, who wryly reported on life in the slow lane, and

Arnold Lehman, who read history, while down the street a mother and daughter were making it, and

Gloria Piano, the plucky swinger, who was making an Olympic effort the second time around, and
Molly Stahl.

When I left the clubhouse after the game, it was dark. As I walked to my car, which was next to a parked security cruiser, I remembered that this was Sunday. I felt depressed — anyone not depressed on Sunday night wasn't paying attention — and I couldn't wait to get home. I had to hurry; time's wingèd chariot was moving faster than ever; I was already losing Lori to nail polish and rock music, to a world where the faces of missing children now came with the milk. This world was a madhouse without doubt: the kidnappers and assassins were hiring agents to make movie deals; but nevertheless I had to be in it, to be out there with Molly and not penned up in a leisure village. The constant pursuit of pleasure was too grim a business for me.

But what about Heritage Village, which was semi-attached to the world? No, I was still too young for even this place. A few weeks ago, Judy had seen me riding my bike in great exuberant sweeps, and she later told me she had thought, *There goes a man with the heart of a child. Also the mind.* And I knew now that a leisure village, even one full of commuting baby boomers, could never be a place for the relocation of this heart.

Come and Rain over Us

PART VII

I n spite of my solemn decision to keep my boyish organs out of adult communities, a few weeks after seeing Heritage Village, I made a social visit to a couple of people at Rainberry Bay, a small leisure village on the east coast of Florida. And there, early one morning, I found myself taking a walk and wondering: if leisure villages did not exist, would they have to be invented? Were they like lawyers or did they fill a basic human need?

While I wandered past the antiseptically nondescript homes of Rainberry Bay at eight o'clock on this morning, I kept hearing voices debate the direction that older people should take.

"Do old folks move voluntarily or does society exert some silent prod to get us into a segregated existence?" Helen Hayes had asked. "Retirement communities are like cute mausoleums, where life is too easy and too bland. When the temperature and sunshine are constant, a kind of boredom sets in that makes each day ooze into the next without distinction."

However, NBC's Joseph Michaels had replied, "Since we live in a youth-dominated world, which has decided that the experience and knowledge we have gained through the years has little value, why not separate ourselves? Why not spend our time talking to people who care about what we have to say?"

And a woman I knew in Maine had answered Michaels by telling me, "A leisure village? Then I'd never see the children walking by to catch the school bus, or the beautiful young mothers on their bikes with the babies behind, or the kids playing lacrosse in my driveway. A leisure village? Why, I even love shoveling out after snowstorms!"

Although I agreed with her, the early morning activity at Rainberry Bay was making me think again about leisure village life. The six tennis courts were filled with doubles players, some of whom knew the game; a few people were riding bicycles, though none of course was doing the fast figure eights that Lori and I loved to make in the parking lot of her school; and coming up alongside me now was a jogger with white tennis shorts, white hair on his bare chest, and a Walkman on his ears. Inspired by his energy, I fell into stride with him.

"Morning," he said, which was either a greeting or part of a lyric.

"If you can hear me," I said, "will you tell me: is this place always so full of morning exercise?"

Baring his ears with a sweep of his hand, he said, "I'm Dave White."

"Hi, Dave, I'm Ralph Schoenstein. You seem like a happy man."

"Damn right!"

"You really like it here, don't you?"

"I couldn't run around like this in *Utica*."

"Utica? I went to college near there: Hamilton. There was a poll in 1950 and Utica came out the worst city in America."

"It's slipped a little since then."

"But you don't do any slipping. You run like a young man."

"I'll tell you something: you feel young just going around in shorts and sneakers all the time."

"Listen, don't let me keep you from the music."

As he switched back to a sound sweeter than my voice, I pondered his theory of sartorial rejuvenation. Here was a man who felt younger merely by *wearing* leisure clothes. Ponce de Leon had never known that he was looking for Calvin Klein.

While Dave continued to circle the grounds, I stopped at the clubhouse pool, where a couple of women were cooking themselves in a Jacuzzi.

"So who'dja see?" one of them said.

"Buddy Hackett," the other replied.

"Oh, he kills me every time."

"Me too, he's hilarious. He did this one routine where he sang, 'Fla-min-go, there's a bird in your ass.' "

"He's the wittiest."

Hearing this talk in the Jacuzzi of Rainberry Bay, I suddenly wondered if my conclusion about leisure villages was in hot water too. I had been deeply impressed by Molly Stahl's freewheeling style in Manhattan, but now I was forced to ask myself: why was it necessarily better for a woman of seventy to dodge dope addicts to hear a chorus chant in *The Birds* instead of taking a Cadillac to hear a man sing about a constipated flamingo? Why was it necessarily nobler to see Strindberg than Shecky Greene? In the JASA dining room, I had been certain of the answer, but my certainty now was ebbing away. My only comfort was the thought that Margaret Mead had gotten Samoa wrong and Fort Lauderdale was just as hard.

In the main clubhouse pool, a grandmother was presiding over the swimming of a small chubby girl, while two other children at poolside were playing Never Talk to a Stranger, the new board game that made kidnapping fun. Watching them play, I understood again the desire to flee a world that inspired such games. And Heritage Village was scheduling the earliest flights.

Walking over to one of the players, a boy about ten, I said, "Do you like it here?"

"Oh, *yeah,*" he replied. "It's really *neat.*"

"Well, just wait a few years. And then you'll be able to move in."